studies that show tremendous successes from rewards, whether they are grades on tests or "play money" that can be used to purchase items at school. The authors place these findings into the broad context of today's changing school environment, increasingly shaped by online learning and choice programs like vouchers and charter schools. They conclude that a realistic understanding of how learning occurs can transform our public schools.

— Jane S. Shaw, President
John W. Pope Center for Higher Education Policy

The authors have analyzed the information available, and they argue that rigorous research shows that properly designed rewards achieve desired changes in behavior, for both students and teachers. I have noticed that Progressive schools which eliminate awards for academic achievement as elitist still keep score in school games, and still pay the teachers. In this work, the authors have suggested a number of reward strategies, some old and some still being tested. This book will surely stimulate yet more useful discussion of the best ways to influence the elusive and essential motivations of the various people (including students) in our schools.

— Will Fitzhugh, Founder
The Concord Review

Through meticulous research, and an engaging writing style, Walberg and Bast have presented the methodology for infusing a rewards system into the classroom, in a way that is both productive for the student, and manageable for the teacher. By offering research driven solutions for incentives, a culture of productivity, motivation, and responsiblilty can be established for children and adults alike. "Rewards" is an excellent read, packed with accessible and relevant suggestions that can be implemented at school, at home, and in the community, as students are driven towards personal, professional, and academic success.

— Heather Wenthold
Director of Curriculum and Assessment
LUMIN Schools

Rewards is a refreshing and comprehensive look at the benefits of using rewards in all areas of K–12 education, including school choice. The authors explain when the government helps break down barriers to parents choosing the best learning environment for their children, it brings lasting rewards for parents and children, and for society as a whole.

— Pam Benigno
Director, Education Policy Center
Independence Institute

It seems so obvious: Rewards motivate us all. The authors clearly refute the research of the nay-sayers to show the positive effects of rewards on motivation when applied to learning. To be most effective on prompting a person to take action or to contemplate the results, educational goals should be SMART: Specific, Measurable, Attainable, Realistic, and Time-bound. To date, too few options exist as rewards on motivation to education; however, Walberg and Bast offer specific, competitive and economical choices to remedy the status-quo.

— Charlene K. Haar, Consultant
Teach-Now.com

Thinking about education – as contrasted with sound educational practice – has been dominated since Rousseau by an unrealistically optimistic view of human nature. The prevailing theme has been that learning should be made intrinsically rewarding, even entertaining, that schools will blossom if teachers would just abandon what is pejoratively referred to as boring drill and kill.

Herbert Walberg and Joseph Bast are by no means opposed to education that is engaging and builds upon the interests of students, but their solidly documented book challenges the naïve belief that intrinsic interest is enough, and the parallel assumption that teachers are so high-minded that there is no need to reward them for efforts going beyond the mediocre routine. Their account of how a variety of rewards function in families as well as in schools is bracingly realistic and packed with practical strategies. It upsets many of the enshrined pieties that have dominated discussion about education.

— Charles L. Glenn, EdD, PhD
Professor, Educational Leadership and Policy Studies
Boston University

From eighteenth century French philosopher Jean-Jacques Rousseau to modern pop psychologist Alfie Kohn, progressives have maintained that children are naturally motivated to learn, and that to offer them achievement incentives demolishes their zest for learning. This well-researched book is a powerful antidote to such fanciful thinking. Walberg and Bast draw from economics and psychology to demonstrate how carefully designed rewards immensely benefit students, parents, and entire schools. Their work is packed with many practical, incentive-based ideas that parents, teachers, and school policy-makers could put to use to boost the quality of education for America's young.

— Robert Holland
Senior Fellow, The Heartland Institute
Author, *Not With My Child, You Don't*

In developing grand education reforms we generally downplay the simple fact that great numbers of students simply won't be interested in cooperating. How to more effectively motivate kids not inclined to do their homework or read assigned books? For their sake and everyone's, please read this path-breaking and invaluable book by Herb Walberg and Joe Bast.

— Mitch Pearlstein, Founder and President
Center of the American Experiment

Rewards

How to use rewards to help children learn – and why teachers don't use them well

Herbert J. Walberg ▪ Joseph L. Bast

The Heartland Institute
www.heartland.org

For my grandchildren, Alana, HJ, and Willa.

— HJW

For Sister Agatha, who taught me how to read and write.

— JLB

Published by The Heartland Institute
One South Wacker Drive #2740
Chicago, Illinois 60606
phone 312/377-4000
fax 312/377-5000
www.heartland.org

Additional copies of this book are available from
The Heartland Institute for the following prices:

1-10 copies	$12.95 per copy
11-50 copies	$10.95 per copy
51-100 copies	$8.95 per copy
101 or more	$6.95 per copy

Printed in the United States of America
ISBN-13 978-1-934791-38-7
ISBN-10 1-934791-38-5

Manufactured in the United States of America

Contents

Part 1. Why Use Rewards?

Part 2. How to Use Rewards

Part 3. Using Rewards to Accelerate Learning

Preface

This book shows how rewards motivate students to learn and how their appropriate use accelerates learning. For some readers this merely confirms the ancient common-sense view that "incentives matter." Children seek praise from adults and strive to win in competitions with their peers while adults work harder for recognition, raises, promotions, and other rewards.

This view has been challenged by popular writers and is controversial in schools of education and teachers' lounges throughout the country. Surprising numbers of teachers oppose using rewards in their classrooms and rewarding teachers or schools for superior achievement. Many of these same teachers oppose tests and using recent advances in digital learning that can more closely align rewards with achievement.

The conceptual framework presented in this book combines principles from behavioral psychology and economics, empirical research conducted in classrooms in kindergarten through 12th grade, and careful studies of the effects of incentives on teachers and school performance. Many rigorous laboratory and field studies by psychologists show how the expectation of rewards or "reinforcements" for reaching goals increases effort and dedication to performing a task well. Research by economists demonstrates how incentives influence behavior as individuals weigh anticipated benefits against their costs in time, effort, money, and foregone opportunities.

While adults are usually paid for their work efforts, it may seem odd to think students should be rewarded or even paid to study or do well on tests. Extensive evidence, though, reveals the power of money as well as non-monetary rewards to influence student learning. Of course, financial rewards are not the only means of motivating young people. Youth invest huge amounts of time and effort in sports and games for their immediate short-term benefits, and they make sizeable sacrifices for altruistic purposes. Some also commit to long hours of demanding study for a chosen career.

We acknowledge early learning takes place socially as parents, teachers, and others encourage children's natural curiosity and innate desire to solve problems. Most children gain satisfaction from pleasing their parents or teachers. They may find learning in itself rewarding. We stipulate that what is rewarding for one student may have little effect on another. But internal motivation alone often isn't enough to help students begin or remain engaged in educational activities. Successful achievers often require personally meaningful rewards to achieve their goals. As they achieve greater mastery, their accumulated skills can become rewards in themselves for continued effort. But until that time, external motivation – rewards – can be crucial.

The hundreds of endnotes in this text refer interested readers to mostly academic research from which the conclusions are drawn. Most heavily weighted are laboratory experiments and randomized field trials in which students are assigned by lottery to either incentivized reward conditions or control groups without rewards. Also included are non-randomized studies that follow students who were similar in socioeconomic and demographic status and in achievement at the start of the research; the studies then contrast the achievement levels of students exposed to rewards with those of students who were not or with those given alternate rewards.

Popular books, news publications, and websites are cited later in the book to show how educators today are successfully using rewards in schools and how innovators are creating opportunities to make rewards immediate, personal, and more precisely aligned with learning progress. We are entering an age of technology and innovation in which rewards can be used more widely, cheaply, and effectively than ever before. All students can be helped by rewards – provided parents, teachers, and policymakers employ well-designed incentives to accelerate learning.

Acknowledgments

The authors thank the donors, staff, directors, and policy advisors of The Heartland Institute who provided valuable support at every stage of this book's writing, editing, production, and release. In particular, we thank Joy Pullmann, Diane Bast, and George Clowes for their research assistance and skillful editing.

Walberg thanks the Koret Foundation and its president, Tad Taube, Hoover Institution Director John Raisian, and Hoover Senior Associate Director Richard Sousa, who supported his early work in planning and drafting the book manuscript. He also thanks Aileen Reid, Winnie Stariha, Trudy Wallace, and Alana Williams as well as his colleagues on the Koret Task Force on K–12 Education and anonymous reviewers for helpful comments on previous versions of the book. They prompted us to transform a dull and scholarly draft into a book we hope is useful to a wide range of readers.

Bast also thanks Randy Piper, a brilliant and unconventional scholar, for lighting a path through the dense thicket of scholarly and popular literature on incentives and motivation. It proved invaluable as we penetrated the deeper levels of the debate over intrinsic versus extrinsic motivation and how it plays out in fields outside of schooling.

Introduction

In the study of human nature, incentives have a long history. Aristotle, for example, distinguished motivational incentives of knowledge, pleasure, and material advantage.[1] Generally speaking, an incentive is a psychological experience that tends to cause greater or lesser effort to achieve an objective. Positive incentives are created by the prospect of rewards, which are usually money, physical objects, states of mind, or desirable actions, while negative incentives are created by fear of punishment or loss.[2]

Some learning is natural, seemingly easy, and may bring pleasure. Learning at the advanced levels necessary for mastery, however, often is difficult and requires diligent study and practice, which is likely to require appropriate incentives. Some students may be motivated primarily by the pleasure of learning, others by the prospects of short-term rewards such as grades, positions in rankings, recognition by peers or teachers, or material rewards such as prizes or money. Others may work hard for the long-term gain they hope will come from professional occupations, while still others may be motivated by a sense of fairness or the opportunity to do good turns for others.

Given the power of incentives to influence behavior, an informed and wider use of appropriate rewards can help students accelerate their learning and acquire knowledge and skills more quickly or at higher levels than they otherwise would.

Why Academic Achievement Matters

Socrates famously said "the unexamined life is not worth living." He was reflecting on the private benefits of learning about ourselves and the world around us. The more we learn about our own thoughts and desires, abilities, limitations, and surroundings, the better able we are to make informed choices about our health, family, occupation, recreation, and myriad other parts of our lives. The non-monetary benefits of learning may be difficult to measure, but they shape and determine what we recognize to be the quality of our life.[3]

Academic achievement produces public as well as private benefits. Eric Hanushek of the Hoover Institution and his colleagues have shown the strong relationship between school achievement and economic growth.[4] Hanushek and former secretary of state George P. Shultz estimate that if our school mathematics scores were comparable to Canada's over the next 20 years, U.S. gross domestic product (the value of goods and services produced in the country) would improve by $70 billion over the next 80 years, a figure equivalent to an income boost of 20 percent for each U.S. worker.[5] That would be a considerable social benefit.

Academic achievement also benefits democratic institutions. When compared to other nations, those with higher levels of education and ability show stronger democracy, less crime, and greater political liberty.[6] Corruption is less common in countries where citizens are well educated.[7]

Within societies, academic abilities increase in step with levels of education, and a nation's relative wealth increases along with both.[8] Cities also tend to grow more quickly when this kind of human capital creates a capable workforce that remains economically productive over time.[9]

Nations tend to benefit to the degree their citizens fulfill their potential. When citizens develop their abilities, liberty tends to expand and moral behavior tends to be higher.[10] Following Hanushek's work, Heiner Rindermann of Germany's Chemnitz University of Technology and James Thompson of University College London found a nation's overall abilities and knowledge are deciding factors in a nation's wealth, scientific progress, and economic freedom.[11] The world's wealthiest nations have sustained strong intellectual traditions that result in notable accomplishments in engineering, mathematics, technology, and basic and applied science.[12] Cross-national studies emphasize the importance of encouraging exemplary learners to achieve as much as they are able. Societies that support top performers and seek to maximize their abilities appear most likely to benefit all their citizens.[13]

Effective primary and secondary schools offer learning opportunities and rewards for acquiring the knowledge and developing the thinking skills students need to succeed in college and workplaces and to participate as citizens in free societies.[14] Longitudinal studies using academic test scores from 90 countries found that despite wide differences in culture, students scoring highest, particularly those in the top 5 percent, also made the largest contribution to their nation's economies.[15] If more students can achieve such levels, they, their compatriots, and their society stand to benefit.

Finally, the quick early learners become ever more knowledgeable and skilled as time goes on, the result of what is called the "Matthew Effect" after this passage in the Bible's Book of Matthew: "For whoever has will be given more, and they will have an abundance." Their work becomes increasingly better than others' and easier for them, which can reinforce their desire and ability to persevere through ever-more-difficult challenges.[16] Academic achievement in elementary and secondary school can foster higher levels of achievement in college and beyond.

Acquired Self-Discipline versus Intelligence
Success in academics and adult life often is attributed chiefly to intelligence, which is presumed to be innate and therefore unaffected by incentives and rewards. But researchers have found academic success is more closely related to acquired self-discipline than intelligence.[17] Discipline, effort, and perseverance all can be changed by incentives. Self-disciplined students who persevere through difficulties tend to gain entrance to better universities and professions and also achieve success in such highly competitive non-academic fields as athletics, the arts, and entrepreneurship, in which winners increasingly tend to take all or nearly all.

The importance of self-discipline and hard work, which some researchers call "grit" or "drive," is a theme to which we will return frequently. The best players in a sport often are not the ones who can throw the farthest or run the fastest, but those who spend many hours studying the game and thoughtfully practicing techniques that lead to winning.[18] This phenomenon may be universal and apply to nearly all human activities, but it is most visible and recognized in sports because the success or failure to acquire skills and knowledge is plainly on display in athletic competitions, whereas failure in other settings often can be hidden or excused by factors other than lack of practice or study. The use of public recognition, trophies, and the right to advance to higher levels of competition is prevalent in middle- and high-school sports programs but is said to be unnecessary and discouraged in classrooms in the very same schools.

The skills and knowledge acquired outside of class competing with peers in high school and college can contribute to success later in life. "The place that best prepared me for college was the hardwood court of men's [high-school] varsity basketball," University of Michigan senior and pre-law major Andrew Snow told *Education Next* recently.[19] He said playing basketball taught him to work with others under pressure, a work ethic, responsibility, and humility. The article quoting him highlighted "a growing body of research" linking after-school activities with high-school graduation, college attendance, and civic responsibility. And indeed this is what the literature shows: Finding and joining constructive activities can help strengthen social networks and compensate for broken homes.[20] Religious and other community organizations such as the YMCA, YWCA, Scouts, and other organizations for boys and girls have traditionally provided such opportunities.

Constructive after-school activities also can help learners acquire the skills they will need eventually to join the adult workforce. Feedback and rewards for specific achievements teach youth about their talents and needs for improvement. Active involvement in civic organizations such as 4-H and Junior Achievement help teenagers learn to plan, communicate, and negotiate.[21]

Overview of Chapters

Part 1 of this book explains why rewards are a necessary part of effective schooling. Support for using rewards was nearly universal in the U.S. until the 1960s and 1970s, when academic and popular expositors such as Jean Piaget, Benjamin Spock, and William Glasser criticized their use on a variety of philosophical, pedagogical, and political grounds.

Chapter 1 reviews the debate among psychologists over the effects of rewards on intrinsic (internal) motivation leading to self-selected choices and behavior. Critics of rewards, under the influence of Jean-Jacques Rousseau and similar philosophers, believe humans, being naturally good, are initially predisposed to be curious and to seek solutions to problems. They are, therefore, internally motivated to learn, but these tendencies are curbed by the invidious influences of parents, teachers, and society. They claim reliance on rewards or extrinsic (external) motivation undermines intrinsic motivation, resulting in less rather than more desirable behavior.

Defenders of rewards counter with theories and evidence that properly designed reward systems do not extinguish intrinsic motivation and in fact can create the conditions young learners need to discover and develop their own goals and learning incentives.

Chapter 2 describes how a parallel debate occurred among economists. Most economists believe rational self-interest and "opportunity costs" (the loss of benefits that would have resulted from a different choice) explain most economic behavior and even a wide range of choices not traditionally thought of as economic transactions. An opposing school claims this model of "economic man" contradicts how real people make choices when confronted with uncertainty. Just as the debate among psychologists resulted in a more nuanced theory of motivation, so has the debate among economists resulted in a better understanding of the role of assumptions in the methodology of economics.

Chapter 3 reviews research on whether rewards really are an effective way to support learning. The chapter concludes that the effectiveness of rewards depends heavily on the circumstances in which they occur. Research shows properly designed rewards are effective in classrooms. The absence of rewards has been shown to have negative effects on student achievement. Critics of rewards focus on instances where rewards were poorly designed or where the research used to study them was unreliable.

Chapter 4 discusses the importance of setting the right goals. Policymakers, educators, parents, and learners themselves all play roles in choosing goals and appropriate rewards for reaching them. We discuss who is best positioned to set goals and how goals and reward systems can best complement one another.

Part 2 of the book shows how to use rewards successfully at home (Chapter 5), elementary schools (Chapter 6), and secondary schools (Chapter 7). These chapters may be of greatest interest to parents and educators looking for examples of how rewards are helping learners of all ages and in diverse school settings. The sheer number of examples and plenitude of research showing their effectiveness should put to rest any lingering doubts as to the effectiveness of properly designed rewards.

Part 3 explores the ways parents, educators, and policymakers can use rewards to accelerate learning. Chapter 8 explains how achievement testing can be paired with rewards to accelerate student learning. Good examples are requiring students to pass tests before advancing to the next grade, providing cash rewards to students for taking or passing optional tests such as Advanced Placement (AP) exams, and providing cash rewards to teachers for helping students pass such exams. Since testing has come under attack by many of the same critics who oppose the use of rewards in schools, we review some of the extensive evidence showing testing is a reliable way to track student achievement and is necessary to provide feedback to learners, teachers, and parents.

Chapter 9 describes research on programs that reward good teachers. We review evidence suggesting large increases in student learning could occur if the behavior of teachers were changed. We show how the current system of paying teachers according to a "single-salary schedule" or "position-automatic system" contributes to the problem of teacher burnout: teachers who feel disrespected, helpless, and trapped in their careers. After reviewing how performance-based pay works in other occupations, we present a series of best practices that apply to its use in schools.

Chapter 10 reports the impressive results of new educational technology that is revolutionizing K–12 schooling in the U.S. and around the world. Digital learning systems solve the biggest challenges facing reward systems: how to tailor the rewards to each student's individual needs and provide immediate and accurate intervention. We describe four successful applications already underway and best practices for policymakers and educators seeking to expand the use of digital learning systems.

Chapter 11 explains how school choice programs can be designed to motivate parents and reward teachers and school entrepreneurs whose schools succeed in raising academic achievement levels. The absence of competition among schools is the major reason so many American educators have made little use of the striking power of rewards documented in earlier chapters. We present four examples of successful school choice programs – KIPP charter schools, California's parent trigger, Indiana's voucher program, and Arizona's education savings accounts – and document their success. Best practices are given for the design of each kind of school choice program.

A brief conclusion wraps up our findings and urges parents, educators, and policymakers to help children learn with rewards.

Notes

1. Aristotle, *Metaphysics*, trans. Joseph Sachs (Santa Fe, NM: Green Lyon Press, 1999).

2. These terms are defined more narrowly in Chapter 1.

3. Luis E. Vila, "The Non-Monetary Benefits of Education," *European Journal of Education* 35, no. 1 (March 2000): 21–32, http://www.jstor.org/stable/1503615.

4. Eric A. Hanushek and Ludger Woessmann, "The Role of School Improvement in Economic Development," *PEPG 07/01*, Program on Education Policy and Governance, Harvard University, January 9, 2007, http://www.hks.harvard.edu/pepg/PDF/Papers/PEPG07-01-Hanushek-Woessmann.pdf.

5. Eric Hanushek and George P. Shultz, "Education Is the Key to a Healthy Economy," *The Wall Street Journal*, April 30, 2012, http://online.wsj.com/article/ SB10001424052702303513404577356422025164482.html.

6. Heiner Rindermann, "Relevance of Education and Intelligence for the Political Development of Nations: Democracy, Rule of Law, and Political Liberty," *Intelligence* 36, no. 4 (July–August 2008): 306–22.

7. Edward L. Glaeser and Raven Saks, "Corruption in America," *Discussion Paper Number 2043*, Harvard Institute of Economic Research (Cambridge, MA: Harvard University, 2004).

8. Heiner Rindermann, "Relevance of Education and Intelligence at the National Level for the Economic Welfare of People," *Intelligence* 36, no. 2 (March–April 2008): 127–42.

9. Edward L. Glaeser and Albert Saiz, "The Rise of the Skilled City," *Discussion Paper Number 2025*, Harvard Institute of Economic Research (Cambridge, MA: Harvard University, 2003).

10. Heiner Rindermann, *supra* note 6.

11. Heiner Rindermann and James Thompson, "Cognitive Capitalism: The Effect of Cognitive Ability on Wealth, as Mediated Through Scientific Achievement and Economic Freedom," *Psychological Science* 22, no. 6 (June 2011): 754–63.

12. Heiner Rindermann, Michael Sailer, and James Thompson, "The Impact of Smart Fractions, Cognitive Ability of Politicians and Average Competence of Peoples on Social Development," *Talent Development and Excellence* 1 (July 2009): 3–25. Knowledge in the humanities, social sciences, and literature may also promote aspects of national well-being, but fair and objective measures in these fields are nearly impossible to develop.

13. Nancy Ewald Jackson and Earl C. Butterfield, "A Conception of Giftedness Designed to Promote Research," in Robert J. Sternberg and Janet E. Davidson, eds., *Conceptions of Giftedness* (New York, NY: Cambridge University Press, 1986), pp. 151–82.

14. Edward L. Glaeser, Giacomo A. Ponzetto, and Andrei Shleifer, "Why Does Democracy Need Education?" *Journal of Economic Growth* 12, no. 2 (June 2007): 77–99.

15. Heiner Rindermann and James Thompson, *supra* note 11.

16. Herbert J. Walberg and Shiow-Ling Tsai, "Matthew Effects in Education," *American Educational Research Journal* 20, no. 3 (Fall 1983): 359–74; Marian J. Bakermans-Krannenburg, Marinus H. van Ijzendoorn, and Robert H. Bradley, "Those Who Have, Receive: The Matthew Effect in Early Childhood Intervention in the Home Environment," *Review of Educational Research* 75, no. 1 (Spring 2005): 1–26.

17. Angela L. Duckworth and Martin E.P. Seligman, "Self-Discipline Outdoes IQ in Predicting Academic Performance of Adolescents," *Psychological Science* 16, no. 12 (December 2005): 939–44.

18. Jean Côté, "The Influence of the Family in the Development of Talent in Sport," *The Sport Psychologist* 13 (1999): 395–417; Jean Côté and John Hay, "Children's Involvement in Sport: A Developmental Perspective," in John M. Silva and Diane E. Stevens, eds., *Psychological Foundations of Sport* (Boston, MA: Allyn and Bacon, 2002), pp. 484–502; Jean Côté and John Hay, "Family Influences on Youth Sport Performance and Participation," in John M. Silva and Diane E. Stevens, eds., *Psychological Foundations of Sport* (Boston, MA: Allyn and Bacon), pp. 503–19; K. Anders Ericsson, Ralph Th. Krampe, and Clemens Tesch-Romer, "The Role of Deliberate Practice in the Acquisition of Expert Performance," *Psychological Review* 100, no. 3 (1993): 363–406; Werner F. Helsen, Nicola J. Hodges, Jan Van Winckel, and Janet L. Starkes, "The Roles of Talent, Physical Precocity and Practice in the Development of Soccer Expertise," *Journal of Sports Sciences* 18, no. 9 (2000): 727–36, DOI:10.1080/02640410050120104.

19. June Kronholz, "Academic Value of Non-Academics," *Education Next* 12, no. 1 (Winter 2012).

20. Michael J. Shanahan and Brian P. Flaherty, "Dynamic Patterns of Time Use in Adolescence," *Child Development* 72, no. 2 (March–April 2001): 385–401.

21. Deborah Bobek, Jonathan Zaff, Yibing Li, and Richard M. Lerner, "Cognitive, Emotional, and Behavioral Components of Civic Action: Towards an Integrated Measure of Civic Engagement," *Journal of Applied Developmental Psychology* 30, no. 5 (September–October 2009): 615–27.

PART ONE

Why Use Rewards?

1

The Psychology of Motivation

The late Jere Brophy, a long-time Michigan State University professor of educational psychology, started the second edition of his 428-page tome titled *Motivating Students to Learn* with the following summaries of two opposing views about how best to motivate students:

> Learning is fun and exciting, at least when the curriculum is well matched to students' interests and abilities and the teacher emphasizes hands-on activities. When you teach the right things the right way, motivation takes care of itself. If students aren't enjoying learning, something is wrong with your curriculum and instruction – you have somehow turned an inherently enjoyable activity into drudgery.

> School is inherently boring and frustrating. We require students to come, then try to teach them stuff that they don't see a need for and don't find meaningful. There is little support for academic achievement in the peer culture, and frequently in the home as well. A few students may be enthusiastic about learning, but most of them require the grading system and the carrots and sticks that we connect to it to pressure them to do at least enough to get by.[1]

Brophy observed that "neither [view] is valid, but each contains elements of truth." They illustrate the two extreme ends of a continuum of views among psychologists of student motivation. At one extreme is a teaching philosophy based on what Brophy called "overly romantic views of human nature," while at the other is a philosophy based on "overly cynical or hedonistic views of human nature." Between these extremes lies a realistic and research-supported theory of student motivation.

Our core message is that too many teachers adhere to the first view and reject the use of rewards that have been proven to be effective in classrooms in carefully controlled studies covering many years and many thousands of students. Critics of the use of rewards in education often rely on misrepresentations of the alternative point of view, often depicting mere caricatures of how psychologists and economists actually view human motivation and the role of rewards in human action.

To be clear, the well-designed reward systems we describe do not include the unearned praise and uncritical recognition associated with the self-esteem fad that swept the U.S. in recent years. Some writers observe that Millennials (persons born from the early 1980s to the 2000s, also called Generation Y) grew up believing that simply participating in a sport or "trying hard" at some other activity entitled them to rewards regardless of their level of performance. As a result, they enter the workforce with unrealistic expectations of recognition, promotions, and pay increases.[2] Greater use of well-designed reward systems would have better prepared this generation for the challenges and responsibilities of adult life.

Rewards need not be crude "carrots and sticks" but can take the form of feedback and encouragement that make learning a *rewarding* experience long before the acquisition of a particular piece of knowledge or skill might earn material rewards. Learning without rewards, we show, is usually more difficult than learning with rewards. For this reason, the tendency among educators to discourage the use of rewards hurts rather than helps students.

What about the feared negative effects of relying too heavily on rewards? Judy Cameron and David Pierce of the University of Alberta said it best when they wrote: "Rewards can have negative effects, but such effects are circumscribed, limited, and easily prevented. A careful arrangement of rewards in educational settings and the work environment can enhance employees' interest and performance. This occurs when rewards are closely tied to the attainment of performance standards."[3] This conclusion, we show, applies not just to employees but also to students.

Extrinsic versus Intrinsic Motivation

USA Weekend, an insert that appears inside millions of American newspapers each weekend, had a cover story in 2013 titled "What Teachers Want You to Know" written by Eric Sheninger, the "award-winning principal" of New Milford High School in New Jersey. At the very end of the article, Sheninger approvingly quotes a teacher giving this advice: "Avoid using rewards and punishments for academic work. If you give your child a dollar for every book he reads, it's less likely he will want to read books for pleasure after you stop paying him."[4] Sheninger and this teacher illustrate the widespread fear among teachers that rewards might extinguish internal motivation.

Psychologists have long distinguished between behavior in response to rewards or "reinforcements,"[5] called *extrinsic* motivation, and behavior arising from internal or *intrinsic* motivation. The possibility that poorly designed reward-and-punishment systems can discourage desirable behavior (as judged by an outside observer) has been long recognized, but experts in the field did not believe this phenomenon was particularly widespread. Most psychologists believed systems involving rewards to influence conduct generally achieved their objectives.

Misleading Research

In 1985, Edward Deci and Richard M. Ryan at the University of Rochester challenged the prevailing wisdom by claiming experimental data showed many reward systems failed to achieve their stated goals.[6] In later works, they maintained that people have three innate psychological needs – competence, autonomy, and relatedness – the fulfillment of which yields enhanced self-motivation and mental health.[7] They argued that compared to extrinsic or "controlled" motivation, intrinsic or "autonomous" motivation more consistently meets these needs, so reliance on intrinsic motivation "predicts persistence and adherence and is advantageous for effective performance, especially on complex or heuristic tasks that involve deep information processing or creativity."[8] Deci and Ryan cited more than 100 studies that seemed to confirm their views.

Daniel Pink, a writer who popularized Deci and Ryan's conclusions, described the implications as follows: "In other words, rewards can perform a weird sort of behavioral alchemy. They can transform an interesting task into a drudge. They can turn play into work. And by diminishing intrinsic motivation, they can send performance, creativity, and even upstanding behavior toppling like dominoes."[9]

In a popular book titled *The Manufactured Crisis*, David Berliner and

Bruce Biddle, both psychologists, relied on Deci and Ryan's research to support their harsh criticism of "programs that use carrots and sticks for motivating students or teachers."[10] "A good deal of evidence now confirms the poor effects of such strategies," they wrote.[11] "Since extrinsic sanctions tend to destroy intrinsic motivation, accountability programs can depress the morale of teachers and administrators."[12] "Perhaps the surest way to RUIN American education," they concluded, "would be to expand the use of carrots and sticks with students and teachers."[13]

The implications of Deci and Ryan's work for education were developed at length by Alfie Kohn, a former teacher and now a popular writer and frequent guest on television and radio shows.[14] According to Kohn, "we are beings who possess natural curiosity about ourselves and our environment, who search for and overcome challenges, who try to master skills and attain competence, and who seek to reach new levels of complexity in what we learn and do." "Incentives simply do not work," Kohn wrote in 1993, and "any approach that offers a reward will fail." The evidence that rewards cause people to do a poorer job on many tasks, according to Kohn, is simply "irrefutable."[15]

Professional educators have many reasons to embrace Kohn's extreme views. Many are persuaded by the extensive research Kohn cites in his books, much of it drawn from Deci and Ryan's work. The underlying philosophy fits a romantic philosophy of human nature popularized by philosophers as far back as Jean-Jacques Rousseau and more recently by Jean Piaget, Benjamin Spock, and William Glasser. Some teachers are simply shamed into embracing the new theory since Kohn and others write that relying on rewards is evidence of laziness or worse.[16]

Definitive Research
Less well known and less welcomed by educators is the mounting body of evidence that Deci, Ryan, and their advocates misunderstand or misrepresent the research they cite to support their conclusions.[17] The strongest critical response to their work came from Judy Cameron and David Pierce, professors of educational psychology and sociology, respectively, at the University of Alberta. In their own meta-analysis of 96 experimental studies, published in 1994, they concluded, "overall, reward does not decrease intrinsic motivation."[18]

In 1999, Cameron and Pierce along with Robert Eisenberger, a professor of psychology at the University of Delaware, conducted another meta-analysis, this time of rigorous experimental studies. They concluded:

> Our meta-analysis found that reward increased perceived autonomy; that reward ameliorated the effects of failure on intrinsic motivation; that reward contingent on meeting an absolute performance standard either increased or did not affect intrinsic motivation, depending on the intrinsic motivation measure used; and that reward contingent on surpassing the performance of others increased intrinsic motivation.[19]

Other scholars have pointed out that many of the studies Deci, Ryan, Kohn, and other critics of rewards rely on had small sample sizes or were poorly designed. For example, most of the empirical research involving control groups involves college students (usually psychology majors) who were given an external reward (credit or grade) to participate in the experiment. As Cameron and Pierce note, "This means that both the experimental and control participants were extrinsically motivated to do the target activity before rewards such as money were offered to the experimental group. One interpretation of this is that much of the research on the topic actually concerns offers of extrinsic rewards for behavior that is already extrinsically motivated rather than the effects of extrinsic rewards on intrinsically motivated behavior."[20]

Many of the studies cited by Deci and Ryan were limited to immediate and temporary states of mind that may not be reflected in performance. The chief purpose of child rearing and schooling is not to make children and adolescents happy but to impart knowledge, skills, and behaviors so they can make informed and wise choices throughout their lives. Long-term control-group studies, rather than quick studies of college students taking psychology courses, ought to form the basis of the debate over the use of rewards in education. Early childhood rewards can yield immediate effects as well as positive effects later in life such as higher test scores in later grades, regular advancement, and greater likelihood of graduating from high school.[21]

Finally, the reward systems being studied run the gamut from unearned verbal praise and trophies for participation to cash rewards for graduating from high school and bonuses and commissions for adult salespeople. The effectiveness of any reward system varies based on its design (for example, how the rewards are explained to participants, when and how they are

given, and whether they are age-appropriate) and other factors. Kohn's
sweeping judgment that "incentives simply don't work" can't be supported
by a careful review of the literature.

Even if reward skeptics were to prevail, what they advocate would be
dysfunctional for occupational life after school completion, which is
substantially driven by extrinsic rewards in the form of employment,
bonuses, raises, promotions, and work recognition. Professionals and
owners of firms are driven by the monetary rewards of serving others well.
Of course, both groups also can be driven in part by intrinsic rewards, but
such rewards may not be sufficient to ensure continuation of their own and
their colleagues' and employees' efforts.

The debate among academics over the effectiveness of rewards resulted
in a range of views. Kohn, Deci, and Ryan are now seen as being at one
end, claiming rewards undermine intrinsic motivation most of the time.
Most other experts say extrinsic motivation can undermine intrinsic
motivation sometimes, due to defects in specific reward systems, but this is
not inevitable or even the common result when rewards are used. Advocacy
of the use of rewards in K–12 education even by behavioral psychologists
such as B.F. Skinner was never as adamant and unconditioned as Kohn and
other critics of rewards imply.

Representing the psychological literature on rewards as a contest
between two extreme views may have been useful and necessary to get
educators and employers to view more seriously the design of the reward
systems they were using. But modern researchers recognize elements of
both intrinsic and extrinsic motivation are likely to be present in most
circumstances.[22] For this reason, motivation research in recent years makes
earlier work by critics of rewards obsolete.[23]

Deferring Gratification

One reason rewards are so powerful is because they teach young children
to defer gratification. Success in later life depends in part on our ability to
wait for greater rewards in the future rather than seize less-valuable
immediate rewards. Those who cannot delay gratification tend to react
thoughtlessly to temptations rather than try to see further ahead to other
possibly larger costs and benefits. Those who can delay gratification tend
to respond to opportunities by making wiser choices that maximize
long-term benefits.

Numerous studies have compared the characteristics of individuals who differ in their ability to defer gratification.[24] The "Marshmallow Test" is an early example of this research. Walter Mischel and his Stanford colleagues told four- and five-year-olds singly that if they could resist eating a marshmallow on a table in front of them for a little while, they would receive two marshmallows. Only one in three children could wait the full 15 minutes before the experimenter returned. Following up 20 years later in the mid-1980s, Mischel found those who could delay gratification were better at concentrating, reasoning, and resisting stress.[25]

Delaying gratification is an important ingredient in "grit," which Angela Duckworth and her colleagues at the University of Pennsylvania define as "perseverance and passion for long-term goals."[26] Duckworth's research showed grit, rather than IQ or prior test scores, predicted academic success as measured by grade-point averages among Ivy League students, retention in the United States Military Academy at West Point, and rankings in the National Spelling Bee.

Child psychologists view deferring gratification as a part of learning self-control. According to Janet Metcalfe and Walter Mischel, the arts of child rearing and teaching depend on extrinsically inculcating intrinsic self-control in four milestones, the first of which is deferred gratification, as shown in the table below.

Milestones of Intrinsic Self-Control

1. Delay gratification, resisting temptation to act impulsively and considering the value of longer-term goals.

2. Balance the need for adult approval and for independence, gaining self-control while considering other people's expectations.

3. Understand the value of material goods, determining why more-important things tend to cost more than less-important things.

4. Enjoy solidarity with others, collaborating as members of teams to achieve common goals and rewards.

Source: Janet Metcalfe and Walter Mischel, "A Hot/Cool-System Analysis of Delay of Gratification: Dynamics of Willpower," Psychological Review 106, no. 1 (January 1999): 319.

Reward systems can be designed to help children achieve all four of these milestones. Self-paced learning programs, especially some of the digital learning programs described later, enable children to monitor their own learning and reward achievement without constant adult supervision and intervention. Programs that give students play money or actual cash for good behavior or taking optional tests teach students the value of things they want and how higher-value items typically cost more time or effort. And teamwork can be encouraged when rewards are given to groups for their achievements, as is common in sporting activities, rather than only to individuals.

Curricular activities that require students to act as if they have self-control can instill the behavior and learning habits that make genuine self-control possible.[27] In a study of minimizing littering and in two studies focusing on acquiring basic math skills, children more often retained their learning when told they were already doing the activities teachers hoped to inculcate.[28] Children who littered were told they are very tidy people who clean up after themselves. Children learning math were told they are able to do the math. Control-group students were merely told they should be doing things the teacher expected. These differences were nearly undetectable to observers but produced significant outcome effects probably attributable to the way students perceive themselves.

Rewards and Learning

According to Aristotle, we become what we do.[29] Education contributes to that process by building skills and habits of mind that are learned in a variety of ways. Psychologists have identified incremental methods for helping individuals learn. Rewards comprise part of this learning enterprise when they help individuals attend to the short- and long-term goals that drive their learning.[30]

When students learn something well, they reduce their costs of doing it; that is, they can use their well-absorbed knowledge or well-practiced skills nearly automatically with little effort. The more automatic a requisite skill is, the faster a person reaches his or her goals. Skills such as recognizing letters exemplify the learning needed to reach the goal of reading. Students who struggle to distinguish a "b" from a "d" are unlikely to readily comprehend what they read. Once they achieve "automaticity" with such recognition skills, however, they can move on to word recognition and sentence comprehension. Mastering the prerequisite stages makes the later stages less costly in time and effort, even enjoyable. Just as practice in sports makes a physical skill more automatic, practice in reading makes a mental skill more automatic.

Students typically must exert effort over some period of time to acquire sufficient levels of automaticity to achieve rigorous goals. Ideally, schooling offers efficient means of allowing learners to improve their knowledge and skills and acquire increasingly advanced forms of both. Educators who use rewards to help learners persist in the face of challenging tasks to gain automaticity also help them reduce the amount of effort needed later to attain their ever more challenging goals. Appropriate rewards improve learners' ability to perceive cues by guiding their attention to constructive action, reinforcing specific forms of learning, and rewarding high levels of achievement.[31]

During learning, repetition can help individuals experience the pleasure of increasingly easy accomplishment. Repeated cycles of presentation, action, and reinforcement can foster high levels of mastery. Complex forms of personal achievement are possible only when individuals set progressively challenging personal goals requiring sustained drive or grit to attain. When the personal goals of these individuals align with those valued in the communities in which they live, they acquire social and material rewards.[32]

Some credibility should be given to theories and evidence that employees may be more effective when they are involved in setting goals to which they commit themselves.[33] Research suggesting students may similarly benefit will be summarized in Chapter 7.

Conclusion

Knowledge of the positive effects of rewards on motivation is well established in behavioral psychology despite the controversy in recent years over whether experimental evidence confirms or rejects the effectiveness of specific reward and punishment systems. Critics of the use of all or most rewards in learning are on the extreme end of a continuum of opinion on the subject. The results of rigorous research studies do not support their points of view, and they overlook or misrepresent research that contradicts their views.

Most experts recognize reward systems are especially valuable at the earliest ages to help students attain the habit of deferring gratification. Failure to develop this habit can handicap learners for the rest of their lives.

Students need rewards to engage in the difficult or tedious work of achieving automaticity, another key step in learning progress. Without rewards, fewer students develop the drive or grit needed to achieve high levels of skill.

Behavioral psychology provides theoretical support for the use of rewards in classrooms. Empirical research that supports this conclusion will be presented in Chapter 3. But first, let's review what economists contribute to the debate.

Notes

1. Jere Brophy, *Motivating Students to Learn* (Mahwah, NJ: Lawrence Erlbaum Associations, Publishers, 2004), p. 1.

2. Ron Alsop, *The Trophy Kids Grow Up: How the Millennial Generation Is Shaking Up the Workplace* (San Francisco, CA: Jossey-Bass, 2008).

3. Judy Cameron and W. David Pierce, *Rewards and Intrinsic Motivation: Resolving the Controversy* (Westport, CT: Bergin & Garvey, 2002), p. 172.

4. Eric Sheninger, "What Teachers Want You to Know," *USA Weekend,* August 23–24, 2013, p. 9.

5. From behavioral psychology, the term reinforcement refers to the use of positive stimuli following behavior that leads to repetition of the behavior. Unlike cognitive and motivational psychologies that emphasize internal states, behavioral psychology emphasizes observable or measurable results.

6. Edward L. Deci and Richard M. Ryan, *Intrinsic Motivation and Self-Determination in Human Behavior* (New York, NY: Plenum, 1985); Edward L. Deci, Richard Koestner, and Richard M. Ryan, "A Meta-Analytic Review of Experiments Examining the Effects of Extrinsic Rewards on Intrinsic Motivation," *Psychological Bulletin* 125, no. 6 (November 1999): 627–68.

7. Richard M. Ryan and Edward L. Deci, "Self-Determination Theory and the Facilitation of Intrinsic Motivation, Social Development, and Well-Being," *American Psychologist* 55, no. 1 (January 2000): 68–78.

8. Edward L. Deci and Richard M. Ryan, "Facilitating Optimal Motivation and Psychological Well-Being Across Life's Domains," *Canadian Psychology* 49, no. 1 (2008): 14.

9. Daniel H. Pink, *Drive: The Surprising Truth About What Motivates Us* (New York, NY: Riverhead Books, 2009), p. 35.

10. David C. Berliner and Bruce J. Biddle, *The Manufactured Crisis: Myths, Fraud, and the Attack on America's Public Schools* (New York, NY: Addison-Wesley Publishing Company, 1995).

11. *Ibid.*, p. 191.

12. *Ibid.*, p. 196.

13. *Ibid.*, p. 194.

14. Alfie Kohn, *Feel-Bad Education and other Contrarian Essays on Children and Schooling* (Boston, MA: Beacon Press, 2011); *The Schools Our Children Deserve: Moving Beyond Traditional Classrooms and 'Tougher Standards'* (Boston, MA: Houghton Mifflin, 1999); *Punished by Rewards: The Trouble with Gold Stars, Incentive Plans, A's, Praise, and Other Bribes* (New York, NY: Houghton Mifflin, 1993); *No Contest: The Case Against Competition* (Boston, MA: Houghton Mifflin, 1986).

15. Alfie Kohn, *Punished by Rewards*, pp. 25, iii, 119, 49.

16. "[I]t takes no courage, no thought, no effort, no patience, no talent, and no time to announce, 'Keep quiet and here's what you'll get.'..." Alfie Kohn, *Punished by Rewards*, p. 16. See also Alfie Kohn, *Feel-Bad Education*, p. 69.

17. For a good overview of the debate and the literature, see Michael Kremer, Edward Miguel, and Rebecca Thornton, *Incentives to Learn* (Cambridge, MA: Harvard University, 2007).

18. Judy Cameron and W. David Pierce, "Reinforcement, Reward, and Intrinsic Motivation," *Review of Educational Research* 6, no. 3 (Fall 1994): 363–423.

19. Robert Eisenberger, W. David Pierce, and Judy Cameron, "Effects of Reward on Intrinsic Motivation – Negative, Neutral, and Positive: Comment on Deci, Koestner, and Ryan (1999)," *Psychological Bulletin* 125, no. 6 (1999): 677–91.

20. Judy Cameron and W. David Pierce, *supra* note 18, p. 81.

21. Arthur J. Reynolds, Judy A. Temple, Dylan L. Robertson, and Emily A. Mann, "Long-Term Effects of an Early Childhood Intervention on Educational Achievement and Juvenile Arrest: A 15-Year Follow-up of Low-Income Children," *Journal of the American Medical Association* 285, no. 18 (May 9, 2001): 2339–46.

22. Martin Ford and Peyton Smith, "Building on a Strong Foundation: Five Pathways to the Next Level of Motivational Theorizing," in Kathryn Wentzel and Allan Wigfield, eds., *Handbook of Motivation at School* (Mahwah, NJ: Erlbaum, 2009), p. 272.

23. Martin Ford, *Motivating Humans: Goals, Emotions and Personal Agency Beliefs* (Newbury Park, CA: Sage Publishing, 1992).

24. An early example is Sharon D. Herzberger and Carol S. Dweck, "Attraction and Delay of Gratification," *Journal of Personality* 46, no. 2 (June 1978): 215–27.

25. Walter Mischel, *Introduction to Personality: Toward an Integration* (New York, NY: John Wiley, 2007).

26. Angela L. Duckworth, Christopher Peterson, Michael D. Matthews, and Dennis R. Kelly, "Grit: Perseverance and Passion for Long-Term Goals," *Journal of Personality and Social Psychology* 92, no. 6 (June 2007): 1087–101.

27. Mark Muraven, "Building Self-Control Strength: Practicing Self-Control Leads to Improved Self-Control Performance," *Journal of Experimental Social Psychology* 46, no. 2 (March 2010): 465–8.

28. Richard L. Miller, Philip Brickman, and Diana Bolen, "Attribution Versus Persuasion as a Means for Modifying Behavior," *Journal of Personality and Social Psychology* 31, no. 3 (March 1975): 430–41.

29. Aristotle, *Metaphysics*, trans. Joseph Sachs (Santa Fe, NM: Green Lyon Press, 1999).

30. See Theresa A. Thorkildsen, Courtney J. Golant, and Elizabeth Cambray-Engstrom, "Essential Solidarities for Understanding Latino Adolescents' Moral and Academic Engagement," in Cynthia Hudley and Adele E. Gottfried, eds., *Academic Motivation and the Culture of Schooling in Childhood and Adolescence* (Oxford: Oxford University Press, 2008), pp. 73–89.

31. Jere Brophy, *supra* note 1; Dennis G. Wiseman and Gilbert H. Hunt, *Best Practice in Motivation and Management in the Classroom* (Springfield, IL: Charles C. Thomas, Publisher, Ltd., second ed., 2008).

32. Julian L. Simon, *Effort, Opportunity, and Wealth* (New York, NY: Basil Blackwell, 1987).

33. Edwin A. Locke and Gary P. Latham, *A Theory of Goal Setting and Task Performance* (Englewood Cliffs, NJ: Prentice Hall, 1990).

2

The Economics of Incentives

Although psychologists commonly write about "rewards," economists most often use the term "incentives." Economic research has long demonstrated that incentives strongly affect behavior in market situations, and like psychology, economics provides insights into and evidence demonstrating how rewards can improve learning in homes and schools.

Incentives in Economics

"Incentives are the pillar of economics and represent everything I'm about," John List, an economics professor at the University of Chicago, told a reporter for *Bloomberg Markets* in 2011. "If you understand the incentives people are operating under, you have a good first guess about what they're going to be doing in certain circumstances and how changes in the environment and/or in their institutions will influence their behavior."[1]

Incentives often arise from competition for rewards. In 1776, Adam Smith anticipated today's debate over intrinsic and extrinsic motivation in education when he observed that "great objects" – the accomplishment of justice or service to humanity, for example – can motivate some people, but such objects "are evidently not necessary in order to occasion the greatest exertions. Rivalship and emulation render excellency, even in mean professions. ..."[2]

The ability of "great objects" to motivate some individual teachers is plainly on display in the accomplishments of Los Angeles math teacher Jaime Escalante or Chicago "miracle worker" Marva Collins, who produced striking results against seemingly impossible odds through strength of character and force of will. But their accomplishments are unlikely to be imitated by others in the absence of institutions that reward such exemplary conduct. As James Taub has said, "any method that depends on a Jaime Escalante is no method at all."[3]

Better than relying on intrinsic motivation, said Adam Smith, is to have people compete with one another for rewards. In a famous passage in *The Wealth of Nations* he wrote, "where the competition is free, the rivalship of competitors, who are all endeavoring to jostle one another out of employment, obliges every man to endeavor to execute his work with a certain degree of exactness."[4] Ever since, economists have been demonstrating how the rational pursuit of self-interest underlies much, though not all, of human action.[5] If choosing a particular option seems likely to produce greater personal benefits than costs, the decision-maker is more likely to choose that option. If the costs associated with the option are greater than the benefits, the decision-maker is less likely to choose it.

The benefits of choosing to act a certain way include what we have been calling rewards or incentives. The costs of a particular action may include time, effort, or money as well as the "opportunity cost" of the decision – the loss of benefits that would have been received had a different choice been made. By studying the costs and benefits of choices, economists can reveal how incentives influence the behaviors of individuals and institutions.

Evidence of the Effectiveness of Incentives

Economists have demonstrated the role of incentives in production and consumption choices for a wide range of goods and services. While they often do not have access to the "gold standard" of a randomized controlled experiment, economists have the advantage over other social scientists of having objective historical data on prices, production, consumption, income, and wealth to test their hypotheses.

The data trail left behind by economic exchanges, sometimes involving millions of people and billions of decisions over periods as brief as a few minutes to as long as centuries, allows economists to view history as a series of natural experiments testing various theories.[6] For example, an anthology of articles on price theory covers the impact of changes in prices on demand for cigarettes, coffee, automobiles, steel, outdoor recreation, durable goods, public education, baseball players, engineers, and scientists.[7] A popular textbook gives examples of changes in the supply and demand for wheat, oil, gasoline, rent, wages, tollway use, and drug-related crime.[8]

Economists study areas of life ordinarily thought to be outside of markets. This effort began in earnest in the 1950s and 1960s by such scholars as the University of Chicago's Gary Becker[9] and Richard Posner,[10] and the literature now covers advertising, art, baseball, charity, child-bearing, crime, dating, discrimination, homosexuality, marriage, religion, and more. Crime, for example, may be economically rational given the monetary benefits and low time costs to the perpetrator and the perceived low probability of apprehension, prosecution, and imprisonment.

In a 1970 book titled *The Gift Relationship*, the late Richard Titmuss argued that monetary compensation for donating blood crowded out the supply of blood donors by extinguishing internal motivation, an early instance of the kind of anti-reward reasoning we described in the previous chapter. His thesis inspired other researchers to conduct scores of studies and write hundreds of articles on the issue. As it turns out, the economics of incentives applies even to blood. A review published in *Science* of rigorous randomized experimental studies and large well-controlled surveys finds money and other valuable incentives have consistent positive effects on people's willingness to donate blood.[11] The research, which documented the use of 14 incentives, including small coupons, T-shirts, and a one-day paid leave from work, showed rewards of higher monetary value had larger effects. Thus, Titmuss was wrong. Similar research has made a convincing case for the use of financial and other incentives in encouraging organ donations.[12]

This literature demonstrates the pervasive power of economic theory to reveal the rational utility-maximizing basis for behavior that at first appears to be irrational or altruistic. It suggests how incentives could be used to encourage desirable behavior in widely divergent areas of life.

Finally, economists use their tools to measure the impacts of government interventions on consumers and producers. Economists have documented the costs and benefits of the entire range of government activities including affirmative action, antitrust laws, gun control, immigration, minimum wage laws, rent control, speed limits on roads, taxation, restrictions on trade, welfare and other entitlement programs, zoning, and even mosquito abatement.[13]

Misleading Research

While economics demonstrates that much of the behavior we observe in daily life consists of rational responses to incentives, economists do not assume that all persons act rationally or selfishly all the time. Nevertheless, claims that the validity of economics depends on an assumption of *homo economicus* or "economic man" date back to the nineteenth century. Modern critics often start by citing the 1981 work of economist Amos Tversky and psychologist Daniel Kahneman.

Tversky and Kahneman reported the results of an experiment involving about 300 college students who were asked to choose among strategies that involved weighing the certainty of gains or losses against the uncertainty of either greater gains or greater losses. The authors noted an asymmetry in the students' choices that revealed a greater aversion to the risk of greater losses than of lesser gains.[14] The study helped launch an effort to find other examples of such behavior – "behavioral economics" – that appear to observers to be irrational and therefore counter to what traditional economics would predict.[15]

More examples were not difficult to find. Dan Ariely, a psychologist at Duke University, conducted dozens of similar experiments on college students and found they made frequent errors when assessing risk and making decisions.[16] In a popular book he described and labeled 11 situations in which his students were "predictably irrational," including "decoys" (college students were easily distracted by a false option), "anchoring" (they searched for benchmarks even when they were obviously irrelevant), and sex (male college students who read or viewed pornography subsequently underestimated the risk of unprotected sex). First-year marketing students and parents of teenagers and 20-somethings would not find any of these results surprising, but Ariely claimed his experiments were profoundly important. He wrote that they contradicted the "assumption of *rationality*" that "provides the foundation for economic theories, predictions, and recommendations."[17] [italics in original]

Bruno Frey, an economist at the University of Warwick (U.K.), also has weighed in over the past 20 years with scores of articles and several books questioning the assumption that people generally make rational decisions. "When people make decisions," he wrote with Alios Stutzer in 2006, "they mainly take salient extrinsic attributes of choice options into account. They thus overvalue characteristics relating to extrinsic desires such as income and status and underestimate those relating to intrinsic needs such as time spent with family and friends and on hobbies. It follows that they tend to underconsume goods and activities with strong intrinsic attributes."[18] In his

1997 book aptly titled *Not Just for the Money: An Economic Theory of Personal Motivation*, Frey claimed "intrinsic motivation is of *great importance* for all economic activities. It is inconceivable that people are motivated solely or even mainly by external incentives."[19] [italics in original]

Two more influential voices in the debate are George Kerlof, a professor of economics at the University of California - Berkeley, and Robert Shiller, an economist at Yale University, who say economics "fails to take into account the extent to which people are also guided by noneconomic motivations. And it fails to take into account the extent to which they are irrational or misguided. It ignores the *animal spirits*."[20] [italics in original] Their book, they write, "accounts for how it works when people really are *human*, that is, possessed of all-too-human animal spirits."[21] [italics in original]

These writers use sweeping claims and lots of italics to persuade readers that conventional economic reasoning had been overturned and is no longer a reliable guide to the role of incentives in behavior. Many of the same educators who embrace the pop psychology claim that external motivation often extinguishes intrinsic motivation also embrace the views of these authors.

Definitive Research

Critics of mainstream economics misrepresent or overlook extensive research that contradicts their views. Their case against the way mainstream economics treats incentives, similar to the case against how mainstream psychology treats rewards, rests on experiments involving small sample sizes and flawed designs. These "laboratory experiments" typically involving college students may be useful to marketers,[22] but determining the effectiveness of rewards in a wide range of areas including learning requires much larger, longer-term, and better-designed experiments.

Economists realize their model of rational utility-maximizing conduct does not provide a complete picture of human nature, but they do not believe this truth invalidates their discipline. Most feel the very lack of realism in the model – its parsimonious use of assumptions about motives and values – makes it more, rather than less, scientific and powerful.[23]

Economists believe the best way to predict the outcome of a transaction is to assume most participants act rationally to attain whatever it is they value. More precisely, the economic doctrine of rational action holds that consumers have stable and ordered preferences and choose the combination of goods that is most preferred at any given time.[24] Ordered preferences imply transitivity: If A is preferred to B and B is preferred to C, then A will be preferred to C. It also implies "more is preferred to less," also called "maximizing behavior."[25]

Nobel Laureate Gary Becker has emphasized "the preferences that are assumed to be stable do not refer to market goods and services, like oranges, automobiles, or medical care, but to underlying objects of choice that are produced by each household using market goods and services, their own time, and other inputs. These underlying preferences are about general aspects of life, such as health, prestige, sensual pleasure, benevolence, or envy, that do not always bear a stable relation to specific market goods and services."[26] This understanding of rational behavior, much different from the caricatures presented by the critics, provides room for economists and psychologists to collaborate on theories of motivation.

Rationality in economics also refers to the outcomes of markets rather than the motivation of individuals acting *in* markets. Markets reward rational action by giving greater control over resources to people who act rationally. When studying markets, it is usually safe to assume rational behavior is the rule rather than the exception, because business owners and managers who do not act rationally tend to produce products and services consumers do not want or at prices they will not pay; consequently, irrational actions lead to the loss of customers and investors. The businesses that survive – the ones we observe – tend to be rationally managed. Most consumer choices, moreover, are rational at least in the sense that they reflect what is preferred and affordable at the time of purchase. To remain employed, workers, too, must usually behave rationally.

Becker emphasizes "the basic demand relations are derived fundamentally from scarcity alone, rather than from an assumption that behavior is 'rational.'"[27] For a typical good or service, the number of units demanded falls as its price rises "even when consumers behave irrationally."[28] Even market critic Robert Kuttner concedes this point: "Even if individual preferences were somewhat arbitrary, unstable, and manipulable, entrepreneurs would remain subject to competitive discipline to offer the best product at the most attractive price."[29]

By focusing on the rational acts of individuals, economists can solve the problem of complexity by assuming as little as possible about people's motives. This is in stark contrast to much of non-behavioral sociology and psychology, where many conflicting theories lead to little agreement in explaining people's behavior. Rather than claim to know or to judge an individual's values, economists speak of "revealed preferences" – those values that are revealed by prices and investment and consumption data each time a consumer chooses one thing over another.

Conclusion

Economists since Adam Smith have argued that most human behavior can be explained by people acting reasonably in response to the incentives they face. They have used "natural experiments" created by changes in prices, supply, and demand to test their hypotheses, resulting in a large body of literature explaining how incentives work.

Financial and other rewards cause many people to exert the additional effort needed to perform at high levels. Economists have quantified those effects and shown how they apply to a wide range of activities that do not normally take place in markets. As we will see in the next chapter, one of those areas is education.

Many of the critics of the use of incentives are the same critics of rewards that we met in the previous chapter, here citing small and flawed "laboratory studies" that show people are not always perfectly rational in their decision-making. But economists don't assume perfect rationality, nor is it required for incentives to work. The application of economics to institutions demonstrates how important it is to allow individuals to make their own choices, even in cases where "experts" claim they know better how those individuals should decide.

Economists, in short, have plenty to say about using incentives. In the next chapter we will look at some of their findings that are specific to education.

Notes

1. Quoted in Oliver Staley, "Professor List's Reality Show," *Bloomberg Markets*, April 2011, p. 92.

2. Adam Smith, *The Wealth of Nations* (Indianapolis, IN: Liberty Press, 1976 [1776]), pp. 759–60. Smith drew from earlier writers including Bernard Mandeville, *The Fable of the Bees* (New York, NY: Capricorn Books, 1962 [1705]).

3. James Taub, "What No School Can Do," *New York Times Magazine*, January 16, 2000, p. 56.

4. Adam Smith, *supra* note 2, p. 759.

5. Edward P. Lazear, "Economic Imperialism," *Quarterly Journal of Economics* 115, no. 1 (February 2000): 99–146.

6. Gerard Radnitzky and Peter Bernholz, *Economic Imperialism: The Economic Method Applied Outside the Field of Economics* (New York, NY: Paragon House Publishers, 1987).

7. Donald S. Watson, *Price Theory in Action* (Boston, MA: Houghton Mifflin Company, 1969).

8. N. Gregory Mankiw, *Principles of Economics* (Fort Worth, TX: The Dryden Press, Harcourt Brace College Publishers, 1998).

9. Gary S. Becker, *The Economic Approach to Human Behavior* (Chicago, IL: University of Chicago Press, 1976). For a more recent compilation of his popular writing, see Gary S. Becker and Guity Nashat Becker, *The Economics of Life* (New York, NY: McGraw Hill, 1997).

10. Richard Posner, *Sex and Reason* (Cambridge, MA: Harvard University Press, 1992), and by the same author, *The Economics of Justice* (Cambridge, MA: Harvard University Press, 1981); *Aging and Old Age* (Chicago, IL: University of Chicago Press, 1995); and *The Economic Structure of the Law* (London: Edward Elgar, 2000).

11. Nicola Lacetera, Mario Macis, and Robert Slonim, "Economic Rewards to Motivate Blood Donations," *Science* 340, no. 24 (May 2013): 927–28.

12. Lloyd R. Cohen, "Increasing the Supply of Transplant Organs: The Virtues of a Futures Market," *George Washington Legal Review* 58, no. 1 (November 1989); Eric Boehm, "Time to Reconsider Cash for Organs?" *Health Care News*, August 2013, p. 14.

13. Anthony Downs, *An Economic Theory of Democracy* (New York, NY: Harper and Row, 1957); James Buchanan and Gordon Tullock, *The Calculus of Consent* (Ann Arbor, MI: University of Michigan Press, 1962); Dennis C. Mueller, *Public Choice* (Cambridge, MA: Cambridge University Press, 1979); and on mosquito abatement specifically, see

Gordon Tullock, *Private Wants, Public Means: An Economic Analysis of the Desirable Scope of Government* (Lanham, MD: University Press of America, 1987).

14. Amos Tversky and Daniel Kahneman, "The Framing of Decisions and the Psychology of Choice," *Science* 211, no. 4481 (January 30, 1981): 453–8.

15. Kahneman won the Nobel Prize in economics in 2002 for his work with Tversky (who died in 1996), despite having never taken an economics course in his life.

16. Dan Ariely, *Predictably Irrational: The Hidden Forces That Shape Our Decisions* (New York, NY: HarperCollins Publishers, 2008).

17. *Ibid.*, p. xix.

18. Bruno S. Frey and Alios Stutzer, "Mispredicting Utility and the Political Process," in Edward J. McCaffery and Joel Stemrod, eds., *Behavioral Public Finance* (New York, NY: Russell Sage Foundation, 2006), p. 113.

19. Bruno S. Frey, *Not Just for the Money. An Economic Theory of Personal Motivation* (Cheltenham, UK: E. Elgar, 1997), pp. 118–9. See also by the same author, *Inspiring Economics: Human Motivation in Political Economy* (Cheltenham, UK and Northampton, MA: Edward Elgar Publishing Ltd., 2001); and *Happiness: A Revolution in Economics* (Cambridge, MA: The MIT Press, 2008).

20. George A. Akerlof and Robert J. Shiller, *Animal Spirits: How Human Psychology Drives the Economy, and Why It Matters for Global Capitalism* (Princeton, NJ: Princeton University Press, 2009), p. 3.

21. *Ibid.*, p. xxv.

22. Richard H. Thaler and Sendhil Mullainathan, "How Behavioral Economics Differs from Traditional Economics," Library of Economics and Liberty, http://www.econlib.org/library/Enc/BehavioralEconomics.html, visited March 10, 2013.

23. Milton Friedman, *Essays in Positive Economics* (Chicago, IL: University of Chicago Press, 1953), pp. 14–5; Gary S. Becker, *The Economic Approach to Human Behavior*, *supra* note 9, pp. 13ff.

24. Herbert Simon, "A Behavioral Model of Rational Choice," *Quarterly Journal of Economics* 69 (1955): 99–118; Herbert Simon, "Theories of Bounded Rationality," in C.B. McGuire and Roy Radner, eds*., Decision and Organization: A Volume in Honor of Jacob Marshak* (Amsterdam: North-Holland Publishing Company, 1972), pp. 161–76.

25. Gary S. Becker, *Economic Theory* (New York, NY: Alfred A. Knopf, 1971), p. 26.

26. Gary S. Becker, *The Economic Approach to Human Behavior*, *supra* note 9, p. 5.

27. Gary S. Becker, *supra* note 25, pp. 21–3.

28. *Ibid.*, p. 25.

29. Robert Kuttner, *Everything For Sale* (Chicago, IL: University of Chicago Press, 1996), p. 42.

3

Rewards and Learning

Research cited in the previous two chapters showed how well-designed reward systems work in a wide range of circumstances to encourage desirable behavior. This chapter reviews research on the effects of rewards on learning in K–12 educational settings. Further evidence will be presented in Part 2 when effective practices are reported and in Part 3 when promising new programs are described.

It is important to acknowledge at the start what the data do not prove. Aristotle elevated beauty above pleasure and material advantage, but any one of these may motivate people to a greater or lesser extent. Some students may be highly motivated to gain knowledge for its own sake while others may be motivated more by the prospects of pleasure or material advantage. Similarly, students in any given class or grade may vary greatly in their responsiveness to immediate and deferred rewards. For example, in Japan students try hard not to let down their small work groups (*han*) within their classes. Awareness of such individual and cultural variations, and using rewards that take them into account, can make incentives more effective.

High-Stakes Exit Exams

John H. Bishop, a professor of human resource studies at Cornell University, has devoted much of his career to studying the effects of high-stakes exit exams on student achievement.[1] He thinks one reason American high-school students don't perform as well as students in other countries is "that they devote less time and intellectual energy to their schooling. Learning takes work, and that work is generally not going to be as much fun as hanging out with friends or playing Grand Theft Auto."[2] Exams with real consequences for college admission and other rewards can cause students to perceive that hard work is worthwhile.

Other countries reward students who score well on high-stakes exams prior to high-school graduation with admission to elite universities and desirable academic programs (such as engineering and pre-medicine). Bishop's research shows the incentives created by such exams raised average achievement by 1.3 grade levels in science and 1.0 grade level in math compared to students in other equally developed countries.[3]

Bishop's research also shows U.S. students living in states requiring them to pass tests before getting a high-school diploma learned more mathematics and science than students who did not.[4] These students were more likely to complete homework, talk with their parents about schoolwork, and watch less television than their peers, all good habits necessary for high achievement. However, such laws, which existed in 17 states in 2004, test only for basic skills and establish a minimum level of academic competence for graduates rather than act as a reward for advanced achievement.

More promising are what Bishop calls "curriculum-based external exit examinations" such as those administered in Canada and other countries and in New York State, North Carolina, and Michigan. These countries and states reward students who score high on more-rigorous exams. "Colleges consider [New York's] Regents diploma a mark of significant achievement," writes Bishop, "making it worth students' while to learn the tested subjects. The Regents exams give students a lofty goal to aspire to, rather than a low hurdle to jump over."[5] Passing the Regents exams is also financially rewarding since high scorers gain free tuition to New York State universities.

Bishop's research on student achievement in several countries shows curriculum-based external exit exams have positive effects on college enrollment, job success, and scores on international achievement tests.[6] They also provide better measures of students' achievement levels than minimum competency tests.

Bishop stresses that not all tests are equal. The ACT and SAT "are not comprehensive measures of a well-rounded secondary education. Both of these admissions tests fail to assess most of the material – economics, civics, literature, foreign languages, and the ability to write an essay – that high-school students are expected to learn. The energy that students devote to cracking the narrow SAT-1 and the ACT would be better spent reading widely and learning to write coherently, to think scientifically, to analyze and appreciate great literature, and to converse in a foreign language."[7]

Paying Students for Test Results

Hundreds of published, well-designed studies, complete with comparison groups, show the benefits of attaching rewards to performance on a wide variety of tests, including frequent low-stakes tests.[8] For example, in 2012, Steven D. Levitt, John A. List, Susanne Neckermann, and Sally Sadoff reported the results of experiments involving more than 7,000 students in three low-performing school districts in and around Chicago.[9] They summarized their findings as follows:

> First, we find substantial incentive effects from both financial and non-financial incentives on test scores. Second, we find that non-financial incentives are considerably more cost-effective than financial incentives for younger students, but were less effective with older students. Third, and perhaps most importantly, consistent with hyperbolic discounting, all motivating power of the incentives vanishes when rewards are handed out with a delay.

Levitt and others' findings confirm insights offered in the previous chapters and that will appear later when we describe reward systems currently working in elementary and secondary schools. For example, financial rewards work better for older students who are "wealthier" than younger students and better understand that money can be used to obtain highly valued things. Rewards should be given as soon as possible to reinforce proper behavior by children who do not yet fully recognize the benefits of delaying gratification.

Small and frequent rewards can keep students motivated to pursue levels of academic achievement that will pay off only much later in life during college or in the workforce. Interestingly, Levitt *et al.* did "not see an increased response of effort when rewards are framed as losses," suggesting the aversion to losses that Tversky and Kahneman first observed in their college students does not apply to younger students or disappears when a larger sample size is used to test the theory.

Paying students for high performance on exit examinations required for graduation can serve as inducements to higher achievement. A program launched in 1999 in Michigan offers one-year college scholarships of up to $2,500 for students scoring highly on the Michigan Educational Achievement Program (MEAP) tests in reading, mathematics, science, and writing. Students in the seventh and eighth grades can receive up to $500 more if they meet or exceed state standards on two of the four MEAP exams. Participation in the MEAP tests rose from 75 percent of seniors in 1999 to 99.7 percent in 2002, average scores rose significantly, and Michigan's scores on the combined verbal and mathematics tests on the SAT-1 rose 5 percent more than for the rest of the country.[10]

Two programs in Israel that reward schools and their teachers with money and additional conventional resources for helping students pass high-school matriculation exams produced "significant gains in many dimensions of students' outcomes. Endowing schools with more resources also led to improvements in student performance. However, the comparison based on cost equivalency suggests that the teachers' incentive intervention is much more cost effective."[11]

More evidence of the effectiveness of financial rewards can be found in Texas, where the O'Donnell Foundation's Advanced Placement Incentive Program offered rewards to students to encourage them to take Advanced Placement (AP) exams and rewards to teachers to encourage them to help the students prepare.[12] AP exams are national tests that provide external, objective, and rigorous standards for high-school students. More than half-a-million high-school students take AP exams on the content of more than 25 college-level courses. More than 2,500 colleges grant course credit for passing grades, allowing students to graduate early or take more advanced college courses.

Beginning with the 1990–91 school year, the O'Donnell Foundation incentive program paid students $100 for each passing score on an AP exam in English, calculus, statistics, computer science, biology, chemistry, and physics, plus a reimbursement for the cost of taking the exam. The program also provided a $2,500 stipend to each teacher undergoing training to teach advanced courses in those subjects. The teachers also received $100 for each passing AP examination score of their students.[13]

In the nine participating Dallas schools, the numbers of boys and girls of all major ethnic groups who passed AP exams rose sharply. The number rose more than 12-fold, from 41 the year before the program began to 521 when the study ended in 1994–95. Those who passed AP courses had a better chance for merit scholarships and entry into selective colleges. Though these numbers speak for themselves, interviews with students, teachers, and college admission officers also revealed high regard for the incentive program. They felt even students who failed AP exams learned better study habits and recognized the importance of hard work for meeting high standards.[14]

Another study, by Lisa Barrow of the Federal Reserve Bank of Chicago and Cecilia E. Rouse of Princeton University, involved 5,161 high-school seniors in California who participated in a field experiment in 2009–10.[15] Approximately half were randomly assigned to a program-eligible group and offered scholarships worth up to $1,300 each semester for two semesters provided they registered for at least six credits and received a final grade of "C" or better. Eligible students were 5.2 percentage points more likely than the control group to enroll or stay enrolled in college, improved their "learning strategies and academic self-efficacy," and "reported studying about 9 minutes more per day than those in the control group, were 7.3 percentage points more likely to have been prepared for class in the last 7 days, and were 6.7 percentage points more likely to report attending all or most of their classes in the last 7 days."[16] The authors also report the students who were offered incentives "were significantly more likely to report behavior consistent with increased internal motivation. In other words, the incentive programs did not seem to reduce their internal motivation."[17]

Paying Students for Inputs

Michael Sandel, a professor of government at Harvard University, echoed the assertions of many other critics of rewards when he cautioned, "if we pay kids to read books, do we simply add an additional incentive to whatever motivations may already exist? Or, do we teach them that reading is a chore, and so run the risk of corrupting or crowding out the intrinsic love of learning?"[18] One of Sandel's colleagues at Harvard, economist Roland G. Fryer, Jr., has done much more than speculate about the effect of rewards on students. He and his colleagues at EdLabs conducted a series of multi-city programs involving cash incentives and found "well-designed financial incentive programs are just as effective as other successful education reforms of the past three decades at a fraction of the cost."[19] In an April 2010 paper for the National Bureau of Economic Research, Fryer explained the incentive program experiments: "In the 2007–2008 and

2008–2009 school years, we conducted incentive experiments in public schools in Chicago, Dallas, New York City, and Washington, DC – four prototypically low performing urban school districts – distributing a total of $6.3 million to roughly 38,000 students in 261 schools. ... The key features of each experiment consisted of monetary payments to students ... for performance in school according to a simple incentive scheme."[20] They tested a wide range of scenarios. For instance, some students received $2 for every book they read; others received $5 for taking a quiz; middle-schoolers could earn $50 if they achieved a perfect score.

Fryer found not every "payoff" was actually rewarding, reinforcing, or apparently worth the effort. An article describing Fryer's work explained, "Most of the students didn't have a clear idea of what to do to 'improve their grades.' Paying students to do things they could control – hand in their homework, read, dress better – did indeed bolster those activities."[21]

Fryer's finding that rewards work best for inputs rather than outputs may seem to partly contradict the favorable results of the O'Donnell Foundation AP program, which rewarded students only for their outputs. However, the outputs Fryer studied were a mixture of intermediate accomplishments and subjective grades rather than actual achievement tests. The O'Donnell Foundation program offered well-defined goals and rewards. Like Bishop's findings reported earlier, the O'Donnell Foundation program shows how well-designed reward programs involving rewards for passing tests can accelerate learning.

NRC Report on Incentives

Some of the findings described above seem at odds with a report on incentives and test-based accountability released by the National Research Council in 2011.[22] More than a few of that report's findings are couched in language that seems designed to minimize or obscure the positive role tests and rewards play in education. It is hardly the final word on the subject, but some of the report's conclusions warrant comment.

The report recognizes paying teachers based on the academic achievements of students changes teacher behavior but warns doing so "can produce dramatically different incentives" depending on what indicators of student achievement are used. For example, a teacher would allocate his or her time differently depending on whether the indicator is average test scores, the test score gains for all students in a class, or the test score gains only for the low-achievers.[23] This is certainly supported by the research we cite and points to the importance of carefully designing such programs. We will discuss this at some length in Chapter 8.

More controversial is this NRC conclusion: "Test-based incentive programs, as designed and implemented in the programs that have been carefully studied, have not increased student achievement enough to bring the United States close to the levels of the highest achieving countries. When evaluated using relevant low-stakes tests, which are less likely to be inflated by the incentives themselves, the overall effects on achievement tend to be small and are effectively zero for a number of programs. Even when evaluated using the tests attached to the incentives, a number of programs show only small effects."[24]

The first sentence sets an impossibly high, short-term standard for judging the success or failure of rewards based on high-stakes tests, the kind studied by Bishop, and is silent on programs such as the O'Donnell Foundation program that reward students who pass AP exams and their teachers. Those incentive programs demonstrated significant improvements in learning in one city, which hardly suffices to erase the big difference between the U.S. and other nations unless widely implemented.

The NRC's observations on rewards tied to low-stakes tests refer twice to results for "a number of programs" but are silent on whether there are successful programs in this arena. In fact there are many, as we will show in the longer discussion of tests with rewards in Chapter 8. Later in its report, the NRC acknowledges this when it says, "The key to using rewards in the classroom is to do so in a way that fosters autonomous motivation. As discussed above, autonomous motivation involves engaging students in a learning activity by helping them identify with and fully accept its importance for their own personal goals and values, even though the activity is not inherently interesting to them (at least initially) and therefore not internally motivating."[25] This comports with our earlier discussion of how rewards can help motivate students to repeatedly practice new skills, such as letter recognition in the case of learning to read, to the point of automaticity so they can master increasingly advanced skills.

Superior Results of School Competition

Studies have shown how increasing competition and consumer choice have reliably increased the quality and lowered the cost or price of a wide range of services including airlines, banks, bus service, debt collection, electric utilities, hospitals, insurance, railroads, savings and loans, utilities, and weather forecasting.[26] Governments have successfully "privatized" (transferred responsibility for delivering a service from the public sector to the private sector) a long list of formerly government-operated enterprises including hospitals, low-income housing, police and fire protection services, and public pension funds.[27] Many authors have written about how the lessons learned in these other areas can be applied to public K–12 education.[28]

Economists and political scientists have found inefficiency and bureaucracy are natural consequences of systems that aren't exposed to competition and consumer choice.[29] Bureaucracies are clumsy, expensive, and often ineffective substitutes for market processes that otherwise reward responsible innovation and punish failure, inefficiency, and laziness. Such inefficiency in public education has been amply documented.[30] A pioneering study by John E. Chubb and Terry M. Moe published by the Brookings Institution in 1990 sought to isolate the role of government operation of K–12 schools in causing this inefficiency.[31] Using a database of more than 20,000 students, teachers, and principals in 500 public and private schools, the authors showed a student's ability (initial student achievement) has the largest influence on the student's subsequent achievement, but "not far behind it in importance are two factors roughly equal in magnitude, the organization of the school and the family background of the student. ... All things being equal, then, it appears that students can really gain a great deal from attending an effectively organized school."[32]

Chubb and Moe found private schools were more likely than public schools to be effectively organized. They tend to have clearer and more academically ambitious goals, principals who are empowered to be educational leaders, coursework that is more academically rigorous, and classrooms that are more orderly and less bureaucratic. "Low performance schools," they wrote, "look less like professional teams and more like bureaucratic agencies."[33]

Public schools, according to Chubb and Moe, are poorly organized public-sector entities subject to interference from and accountable to elected bodies, what they call "democratic control." In a remarkably blunt summary of their findings, Chubb and Moe wrote:

> The way to get schools with effective organizations is not to insist that democratic institutions should do what they are incapable of

doing. Nor is it to assume that the better public schools, the lucky ones with nice environments, can serve as organizational models for the rest. Their luck is not transferable. The way to get effective schools, rather, is to recognize that the problem of ineffective performance is really a deep-seated institutional problem that arises from the most fundamental properties of democratic control.[34]

The alternative to democratic control is competition and choice: requiring that schools compete among themselves for students and tuition while allowing parents to select the schools they believe are best for their children. Competition rewards school administrators and teachers who work together to produce high-quality outcomes without wasting resources. Unlike monopolies, competitive markets allow producers to specialize and differentiate their products and services, giving consumers more options and choices that are likely to satisfy their wants.

While competition and choice in public K–12 education is highly constrained, enough exists to allow scholars to estimate their effects on student achievement and other outcomes. That research generally compares outcomes of traditional public schools with four kinds of schools exposed to competition: private schools, charter schools, schools participating in public voucher programs, and public schools that compete with one another due to small district sizes or open enrollment policies. Researchers have focused on changes in five measurable outputs of schools attributable to the incentives created by competition and choice. The five outputs are:

- point-in-time academic achievement, meaning the academic standing of students (such as test scores, graduation rate, and college enrollment after graduation) attending schools of choice versus traditional public schools, usually using statistical methods to control for differences in students' socioeconomic status;

- value-added over-time achievement gains, which controls for possible selection bias by taking into account a student's level of achievement *before* attending a school of choice and measuring only the increase (or decrease) attributable to the school;

- cost efficiency, typically annual spending per student, an estimate that is sometimes complicated by differences between tuition and actual spending for private schools and per-pupil spending by public schools reported by teachers unions versus more inclusive measures reported by independent researchers;[35]

■   parental satisfaction or citizens' favorable regard, as revealed by surveys of parents and the general public; and

■   social integration or citizenship, as revealed by the diversity of student bodies, surveys of students asking how frequently they interact with students of different ethnicities, scores on civics exams, and levels of student participation in voluntary civic activities.

A comprehensive survey of research on these effects of school choice conducted in 2007 found near-consensus support for the proposition that school choice has positive effects on students attending all four types of schools and for all five types of outcomes under investigation.[36] A table summarizing the research appears below.

As shown by the table, the evidence is conclusive for 14 of the 20 findings and suggestive-but-not-conclusive for the remaining six. Given the uncertainties inherent in social science research, this is dramatic and compelling evidence that competition among schools benefits students, satisfies parents and citizens, and improves efficiency.

Survey of the Evidence for Positive School Choice Effects					
Form of Choice	Point-in-time academic achievement	Value-added-over-time achievement gains	Cost efficiency	Parental satisfaction, citizens' favorable regard, or both	Social integration, citizenship, or both
Charter schools	Conclusive	Conclusive	Conclusive	Conclusive	Suggestive
Vouchers	Conclusive	Conclusive	Conclusive	Conclusive	Suggestive
Private schools	Conclusive	Suggestive	Conclusive	Conclusive	Conclusive
Competition	Conclusive	Suggestive	Suggestive	Conclusive	Suggestive
Source: Herbert Walberg, *School Choice: The Findings* (Washington, DC: Cato Institute, 2007), Table 7-1, p. 108.					

Conclusion

The use of rewards to motivate students to learn has been studied extensively. Contrary to the views of some prominent skeptics, the effectiveness of rewards has been amply demonstrated. Successful programs reward students for doing well on optional high-stakes and mandatory exit exams, for enrolling in AP courses and passing the exams, and for inputs such as reading books, coming to class on time, and turning in homework.

Not every reward program works. Wise educators (and parents) know the effectiveness of rewards depends on the learner, the situation, and the design of the reward system. Rewards appropriate for young children may not be appropriate for older students; rewards for accomplishments that seem out of reach or that arrive months or years later are likely to fail; and reward systems that don't align with or respect the student's own interests, knowledge, and needs are unlikely to work.

Research shows how the absence of rewards built into the current organization of public K–12 schools makes it more difficult for conventional schools to organize for success and perform well. Schools that are insulated from competition can afford to operate "like bureaucratic agencies." Incentives matter for teachers and administrators, too.

The good news is that many years of experience and hundreds of articles in scholarly journals can help parents, educators, and policymakers design reward systems that achieve their objectives. The research in this chapter, combined with the previous two describing the underlying psychological and economic theories and evidence, makes a compelling case for increasing the use of well-designed rewards in schools.

Notes

1. John H. Bishop, Joan Y. Moriarty, and Ferran Mane, "Diplomas for Learning, Not Seat Time: The Impacts of New York Regents Examinations," *Economics of Education Review* 19, no. 4 (October 2000): 333–49; John H. Bishop, "The Effect of National Standards and Curriculum-based Exams on Achievement," *The American Economic Review* 87, no. 2 (May 1997).

2. John H. Bishop, "Money and Motivation," *Education Next*, January 2004.

3. John H. Bishop, "Curriculum-Based External Exam Systems: Do Students Learn More? How?" *Psychology, Public Policy, and Law* 6, no. 1 (March 2000): 199–215. See also Richard Phelps, ed., *Defending Standardized Testing* (Mahwah, NJ: Lawrence Erlbaum Associates Publishers, 2005).

4. John H. Bishop, *ibid.*

5. *Ibid.*

6. John H. Bishop, Ferran Mane, and Michael Bishop, "How External Exit Exams Spur Achievement," *Educational Leadership* 59, no.1 (September 2001): 58–63.

7. John H. Bishop, *supra* note 2.

8. Herbert J. Walberg, *Tests, Testing, and Genuine School Reform* (Stanford, CA: Education Next Books, 2011).

9. Steven D. Levitt, John A. List, Susanne Neckermann, and Sally Sadoff, "The Behavioralist Goes to School: Leveraging Behavioral Economics to Improve Educational Performance," *NBER Working Paper No. 18165*, June 2012, http://www.nber.org/papers/w18165. Quotations are from the abstract.

10. *Supra* note 2.

11. Victor Lavy, "Performance Incentives on Pupil Achievement," *Journal of Political Economy* 110, no. 6 (December 2002): 1286.

12. Visit http://www.apstrategies.org/IncentivePrograms/OurResults.aspx to see the latest numbers for students participating in the program.

13. C. Kirabo Jackson, "Cash for Test Scores: The Impact of the Texas Advanced Placement Incentive Program," *Education Next* 8, no. 4 (Fall 2008). See also Herbert J. Walberg, "Incentivized School Standards Work," *Education Week*, November 4, 1998, p. 48.

14. C. Kirabo Jackson, *ibid.*

15. Lisa Barrow and Cecilia Rouse, "Financial Incentives and Educational Investment: The Impact of Performance-Based Scholarships on Student Time Use," *NBER Working Paper No. 19351*, August 2013, http://www.nber.org/digest/dec13/w19351.html.

16. *Ibid.*, pp. 20–22.

17. *Ibid.*, p. 23.

18. Michael Sandel, "If I Ruled the World," *Prospect*, September 19, 2012, http://www.prospectmagazine.co.uk/economics/if-i-ruled-the-world-michael-sandel/. He recites this and virtually all the other erroneous objections to economics and incentives we've discussed in *What Money Can't Buy: The Moral Limits of Markets* (New York, NY: Farrar, Straus and Giroux, 2012).

19. Ed Labs: The Education Innovation Laboratory at Harvard University, "Innovations," http://www.edlabs.harvard.edu/.

20. Roland G. Fryer, "Financial Incentives and Student Achievement: Evidence from Randomized Trials," National Bureau of Economic Research, *NBER Working Paper No. 15898*, April 2010, p. 38, http://citeseerx.ist.psu.edu/viewdoc/summary?doi=10.1.1.169.6593.

21. EdSurge, "Personal Tutors And Paying For Good Grades: Roland Fryer's Experiments On Children," Co.Exist FastCompany, February 8, 2012, http://www.fastcoexist.com/1679290/roland-fryer-education-innovation-laboratory.

22. Michael Hout and Stuart W. Elliott, eds., *Incentives and Test-Based Accountability in Education*, National Research Council (Washington, DC: The National Academies Press, 2011).

23. *Ibid.*, p. 3.

24. *Ibid.*, p. 4.

25. *Ibid.*, p. 30.

26. Charles Wolf, Jr., *Markets or Governments: Choosing Between Imperfect Alternatives* (Cambridge, MA: The MIT Press, 1988); E.S. Savas, *Privatization and Public Private Partnerships* (New York, NY: Chatham House Publishers, 2000).

27. Leonard Gilroy and Adrian Moore, "Privatization," Chapter 4 of *The Patriots Toolbox*, 3rd revised edition (Chicago, IL: The Heartland Institute, 2011), pp. 119–47.

28. Myron Lieberman, *Privatization and Educational Choice* (New York, NY: St. Martin's Press, 1989); Henry M. Levin, ed., *Privatizing Education* (Boulder, CO: Westview Press, 2001); Herbert J. Walberg, "Uncompetitive American Schools: Causes and Cures," in Diane Ravitch, ed., *Brookings Papers on Education Policy* (Washington, DC: Brookings Institution, 1998), pp. 173–255.

29. James Q. Wilson, *Bureaucracy: What Government Agencies Do And Why They Do It* (New York, NY: Basic Books, 1991); Gordon Tullock, *Bureaucracy: The Selected Works of Gordon Tullock, Volume 6*, Charles K. Rowley, ed. (Indianapolis, IN: Liberty Fund, 2005).

30. National Commission on Excellence in Education, *A Nation at Risk* (Washington, DC: U.S. Department of Education, 1983); Jay P. Greene, *Education Myths* (Lanham, MD: Rowman & Littlefield Publishers, Inc., 2005); Myron Lieberman, *Public Education: An Autopsy* (Cambridge, MA: Harvard University Press, 1995), and by the same author, *The Educational Morass: Overcoming the Stalemate in American Education* (Lanham, MD: R&L Education, 2007).

31. John E. Chubb and Terry M. Moe, *Politics, Markets and America's Schools* (Washington, DC: Brookings Institution,1990).

32. *Ibid.*, p. 129.

33. *Ibid.*, p. 91.

34. *Ibid.*, p. 191.

35. Myron Lieberman and Charlene K. Haar, *Public Education as a Business: Real Costs and Accountability* (Oxford, UK: Scarecrow Press, Inc., 2003); Adam B. Schaeffer, "They Spend WHAT? The Real Cost of Public Schools," *Policy Analysis No. 662*, Cato Institute, March 10, 2010, http://www.cato.org/pub-display.php?pub-id=11432.

36. Herbert J. Walberg, *School Choice: The Findings* (Washington, DC: Cato Institute, 2007).

4

Setting the Right Goals

An important early step in using incentives to accelerate learning is understanding the goals set for, and sometimes by, learners. Clear agreed-upon goals allow educators to concentrate on planning the best way to bring them about rather than deliberating about what they should be. America's cultural diversity and unique heritage make this difficult for conventional public schools.

What are the features of effective goals, who should choose them, and how do goals relate to aspects of learning that are best left unplanned and spontaneous?

Features of Effective Goals

Early learning is a social act that can involve parents, siblings, teachers, and others. Social incentives alone, however, are insufficient for keeping individuals engaged in many types of educational activities. Together with incentives, goals help students focus on the specific activities that help them succeed.[1] Incentives aligned with goals help learners choose the best options from an array of possible activities and direct their efforts toward attaining the most valuable outcomes.[2] Material and social incentives work well in some circumstances while some activities are self-reinforcing; the effort itself may be enjoyable and inspire sustained effort.[3]

In reviewing many studies of incentives in varied adult settings, University of Maryland psychologist Edwin Locke and his colleagues concluded that setting specific, challenging goals leads to higher performance than setting easy goals, "do your best" goals, or no goals.[4]

"Goals," they further concluded, "affect performance by directing attention, mobilizing effort, increasing persistence, and motivating strategy development. Goal setting is most likely to improve task performance when the goals are specific and sufficiently challenging ... feedback is provided ... the experimenter or manager is supportive, and the assigned goals are accepted by the individual."

Thus, psychological research supports the view that effective goals are "SMART"; that is, Specific, Measurable, Attainable, Realistic, and Time-bound.[5] Individuals guided by such goals are more likely to sustain a commitment to the tasks at hand. More broadly, goals allow people to imagine personal and social outcomes likely to emerge from sustained effort. Skilled goal-directed individuals can imagine the complexity of their task with some degree of accuracy and determine the sort of intermediate feedback that might best foster successful attainment of the goal. They may fail to achieve their goals for a variety of reasons and may need to revise their goals, but in such situations incentives can encourage individuals to keep trying.

Who Should Set the Goals?

Children attending preschool and elementary schools are too young to decide on their own what they should learn since they lack sufficient understanding of the importance and consequences of their choices. Few would disagree that adults should take responsibility for setting young children's long- and short-term curriculum goals. Even so, controversy has emerged over who should set the goals, whether people can agree on them, and how to hold schools, educators, and students accountable for meeting them. This makes setting goals and incentives difficult not just for very young children but for all K–12 students.

Many Asian and European countries have national standards for schools that spare all but a small number of educators the time and difficulty of deciding the contents of K–12 curriculum. Such standardization facilitates the development of uniform textbooks and methods of teaching and testing and makes it more likely that all children in any given classroom have similar levels of knowledge and skills. Such standardization also allows policymakers and parents to hold schools accountable for results by having all students take the same or a similar set of achievement tests.

Though appealing, a national curriculum and centralized system of student testing is a poor fit for K–12 schools in the U.S. The small number of decision-makers that may make the process seem efficient excludes stakeholders such as parents with strong interests and legally recognized rights to play a role in the education of children. The sheer size and cultural diversity of the country's population create a variety of deeply rooted and fiercely held views on what ought to be taught in schools. This disagreement is most plainly on display in controversies over the teaching of history, religion, ethics, and matters involving public policy, but it extends to ways of teaching reading (phonics versus whole word) and arithmetic (traditional versus "fuzzy math"). As the controversy over adoption of "Common Core" standards as part of the national "Race to the Top" federal initiative demonstrates,[6] there isn't one best curriculum for the U.S.

The lack of consensus on goals for K–12 education in the U.S. was addressed by the Founding Fathers by excluding education from the enumerated powers of the national government; the words "education" and "schools" do not appear in the Constitution. The authority to regulate schooling was delegated by the Tenth Amendment to the states. For nearly a century the states entrusted the private sector with operating schools. Later, compulsory attendance laws and the Common School movement of the mid-nineteenth century left education policy in the hands of cities and local communities. This accommodation has the virtue of allowing innovation and competition among cities and states, an essential condition for discovery and improvement. It also made it difficult for large state and national interest groups to gain control over school goals and curricula.

While the current system is far from perfect, there is little public support for giving the federal government more authority over schools. From 1973 to mid-2010, the percentage of Americans expressing "a great deal" or "a lot" of confidence in Congress declined from 42 percent to 11 percent, ranking it last among 16 familiar institutions including small business, the police, religious institutions, and the medical system.[7] Opportunities for improving goal-setting for K–12 schools, therefore, are most likely to be found at the state and local levels or outside of government altogether.

Parents and Goal-setting

Parents may be considered the most important part of the goal-setting team since they have a constitutionally protected right to control the education of their children.[8] The most notable of many Supreme Court decisions establishing this right is the 1925 decision in *Pierce v. Society of Sisters* in which the court ruled "The child is not the mere creature of the state; those who nurture him and direct his destiny have the right, coupled with the high duty, to recognize and prepare him for additional obligations."

Parents are better positioned than teachers, school board members, or members of Congress to know their children's specific needs, interests, and talents.[9] They are least likely to have a conflict of interest – where their private interests might conflict with the interests of the child – since they are not paid for their services nor are they running for election or reelection based on claims or promises made about the education of other people's children. Parents' future well-being is tied to the ability of their children to become self-supporting and law-abiding adults.[10]

About 90 percent of the time in a child's first 18 years of life is spent outside schools under the responsibility of parents, including the parental surrogates and others they may choose for their children. Parents teach many of the most important lessons in life including manners, attitudes toward school and learning, and the all-important first language. Homework by definition is done at home and is influenced by parents. For these reasons, it is important for parents to know and embrace the broad goals of their children's schools and for schools in turn to reflect the concerns and interests of parents.

Good teachers should play a role in setting academic goals for students, but they face conflicts of interest. Margaret Diane LeCompte and Anthony Gary Dworkin, who self-identify as "progressive" educators, nevertheless observe, "teachers generally do not believe that parents will provide adequate support for their children's learning at home. Further, many teachers – whether consciously or not – act in ways that sabotage efforts by parents to help their children."[11] They observe "most teachers" withhold information from parents when their children are doing poorly, "even when it is apparent that they are," in order to discourage complaints or requests for help that might involve spending more time with struggling students or their parents. Teachers may do this unconsciously: "Because many parents have unrealistically optimistic perceptions of their children's progress, they do not seek help for them. By failing to ask for help, they demonstrate to teachers their 'lack of interest.'"[12] But regardless of the reason behind the teachers' failure to communicate, their silence inflicts serious harm on children, leaving them unprepared for work at the next grade level or even, in some cases, forcing them to go through the shame of having to repeat a grade.

The need to align school offerings with parents' interests and values, combined with the recognition that conflicts of interest afflict even well-meaning and dedicated teachers, makes a compelling case for allowing schools to offer a diversity of curricula and education philosophies and for enabling parents to be free to choose schools they believe are best for their children.[13]

State and Local Goal-setting

Second to parents, state and local officials presently play the most important roles in setting goals for K–12 learning. Governors, other state elected officials, and state and local school board members spend countless hours planning and overseeing public schools, a massive public enterprise that cost taxpayers at least $571 billion for the 2012–13 school year.[14] Over time, control over public education has been concentrated in fewer and fewer hands: the number of districts shrank from about 117,000 in 1940 to 15,000 in 2000, while the average enrollment in a district rose from 217 children to more than 3,000 children.[15]

On the matter of goal-setting, state and local officials have attempted to set high and uniform achievement goals combined with top-down accountability systems requiring that only the approved curriculum is taught and students advance at an acceptable pace.[16] In some states, teachers who fail to teach the approved curriculum or whose students don't advance fast enough receive training, face disciplinary action, or receive financial incentives to improve their performance. Schools that repeatedly fail to meet the standards are subject to top-down reorganization by state authorities. "Turnaround" and "transformation" are two kinds of reorganization prescribed by Race to the Top, the national school legislation adopted in 2009.[17]

The turnaround model requires a local school district to "replace the principal and grant the new principal sufficient operational flexibility (including in staffing, calendars/time, and budgeting) to implement a comprehensive approach in order to substantially improve student achievement outcomes and increase high-school graduation rates." The new approach includes screening existing staff, rehiring no more than 50 percent of them, hiring a "turnaround leader," and promoting "the continuous use of student data (such as from formative, interim, and summative assessments) to inform and differentiate instruction in order to meet the academic needs of individual students."[18]

The transformation model is similar to the turnaround model but adds a dozen additional reform options such as "conducting periodic reviews to ensure that the curriculum is being implemented with fidelity, is having the intended impact on student achievement, and is modified if ineffective" and "increasing rigor by offering opportunities for students to enroll in advanced coursework (such as Advanced Placement or International Baccalaureate; or science, technology, engineering, and mathematics courses, especially those that incorporate rigorous and relevant project-, inquiry-, or design-based contextual learning opportunities), early-college high schools, dual enrollment programs, or thematic learning academies that prepare students for college and careers, including by providing appropriate supports designed to ensure that low achieving students can take advantage of these programs and course work."[19]

Turnaround and transformation seem to be tough-minded and business-like approaches to the task of setting goals and achieving results. They are the current state-of-the-art of the public school reform industry. But do they work? Experience with turnaround efforts suggests they do little to increase student achievement and parent satisfaction with schools.[20] For example, a U.S. Department of Education evaluation of schools that spent $4.6 billion on transformations or turnarounds found only a quarter of them experienced significant math or reading gains while three-quarters made little or no progress.[21]

Turnaround and transformation efforts often fail because they leave in place the centralized district authority and bureaucracy that have pushed parents out of their children's education, reducing their involvement and consequently reducing their children's academic achievement. For the most part the efforts don't change the incentives that currently distract and frustrate good teachers and administrators. They repeat the top-down and one-size-fits-all reform prescriptions that large bureaucracies use in lieu of having to compete with other providers for customers. Consequently, these reforms will be implemented slowly and imperfectly, if at all, and teachers and administrators will find ways to evade and circumvent the new rules ... sometimes to hide their incompetence, and at other times to do what parents and students actually want and need.

Goals and Spontaneous Order
People in academia and government often assume "experts" uninvolved in

the daily life of others can best set goals for them.[22] This model may sometimes prove successful if the goal setter possesses extensive experience with unchanging goals and knowledge of the circumstances and experiences of others, but more typically a single person or organization lacks the information required for seeing and pursuing someone else's goals.[23] Some degree of spontaneity rather than complete pre-ordering of options can cultivate innovative thought or new ways of looking at problems.[24]

Some prominent Chinese citizens voice concern about their country's highly structured education system. They worry that too much planning crushes natural instincts for innovation and creativity necessary for a vibrant culture and economy.[25] Some South Koreans express similar concerns about their education system, which has a substantially longer year and longer school days than the U.S. school system. Their culture focuses so exclusively on academic achievement that some South Korean parents choose to exempt their children from the pressure by sending them to American schools in Korea. These parents say students at American schools have more opportunities to explore extracurricular activities and develop outside interests.[26] Some balance between planning and spontaneity, or strict and open-ended goals, is needed. That balance varies among countries, schools, families, and students.

As students grow older they begin taking control of their learning progress. A competitive and thriving marketplace of ideas, even in classrooms, may help students learn to evaluate new ideas that may not be found in textbooks. Surfing the Internet confronts young learners with new and potentially false ideas and claims that deserve consideration and evaluation, which is good practice since judging the veracity of information is an important life skill. Not all judgments and decisions can be taught or reduced to methodical textbook recipes.[27]

Without this freedom to explore, some learners set goals that limit their ability to learn new ways of evaluating ideas, while others continually seek these skills and thereby improve their understanding and functioning in the world.[28] Too little structure or guidance, though, can lead some learners to become so anxious and self-conscious in the face of uncertainty that they cannot concentrate on evaluating unanticipated parts of the task at hand.[29] Well-planned goals and rewards help learners avoid distractions and achieve what they wish as well as evaluate new ideas and, if necessary, redirect their efforts.

Another problem of top-down goal-setting is unpredictable events that slow down or even terminate complex projects. Supervisors, for example, often incorrectly estimate difficulty and how long it will take to complete tasks.[30] Information technology professionals sometimes joke that planners should make the best estimate of the time required to finish a project and multiply it by three – five if computers are involved. Many complex projects go unfinished because time, resources, and patience are depleted or a superior technology eclipses what was envisioned.[31]

Public education is certainly a complex project. Policymakers spend years debating and approving curricula and other school policies that are obsolete by the time they reach classrooms. Teacher contracts and laws governing schools and school finance can reach the size of phone books, making even small changes at the level of individual schools difficult and time-consuming to make.[32] The digital revolution is occurring outside traditional public schools, which trail far behind the cutting edge.[33]

Education today is, in short, an enterprise that seems particularly ill-suited to top-down goal-setting even if there were agreement on what the goals should be, which there manifestly is not. This is a fundamental problem in public education that needs to be solved before effective reward programs can be widely adopted.

Conclusion

The right goals must be chosen before incentives can be used effectively in education, but setting goals for individual learners is more difficult than many people realize. America's unique political heritage means there are deep differences of opinion on what should be taught in K–12 schools beyond basic agreement on the three Rs. These disagreements are not primarily between people who understand complex subjects and those who do not; they are rooted in cultures, experiences, and belief systems that are accepted and celebrated as part of the American Way, or rather the American Ways.

One implication of our cultural diversity and enthusiastic embrace of the same is that the federal government has only a small role to play in setting goals for K–12 education. Responsibility rests primarily with parents, state and local governments, and school boards. This choice has both advantages – there is more innovation, competition, and freedom to choose thanks to decentralization – and disadvantages – more time spent debating goals and teaching practices, and a lack of uniform textbooks and uniform tests with which to hold educators and students accountable to a single standard. This is not to say, however, that parents should be denied accurate information on what their children are learning and where they stand in relation to their peers on important subjects such as English, American history, mathematics, and science.

Goal-setting should not be viewed as a straitjacket, preventing learners from exploring new ideas or altering goals over time. Adults, even parents, cannot know everything going on in a child's mind. While adults have essential roles to play in goal-setting for young children, their roles evolve as children grow older. As discussed in earlier chapters, goals and incentives need to change to reflect the learner's increased maturity and thinking skills.

In light of all this, perhaps the best that can be hoped for is that educators, parents, and students themselves will have a hand in goal-setting and creating incentive systems. It can be a difficult balancing act requiring the best efforts of everyone involved.

Notes

1. James T. Austin and Jeffrey B. Vancouver, "Goal Constructs in Psychology: Structure, Process, and Content," *Psychological Bulletin* 120, no. 3 (November 1996): 338–75.

2. Barry J. Zimmerman and Manuel Martinez-Pons, "Construct Validation of a Strategy Model of Student Self-Regulated Learning," *Journal of Educational Psychology* 80, no. 3 (September 1988): 284–90.

3. Mihaly Csikszentmihalyi, *Flow: The Psychology of Optimal Experience* (New York, NY: Harper and Row, 1990).

4. Edwin A. Locke, Karyl N. Shaw, Lise M. Saari, and Gary P. Latham, "Goal Setting and Task Performance: 1969–1980," *Psychological Bulletin* 90, no. 1 (July 1981): 125–52.

5. For a popular description of the SMART approach and applications to everyday life, see the "Mind Tools" site at http://www.mindtools.com/page6.html.

6. Joy Pullmann, "The Common Core: A Poor Choice for States," *Policy Brief*, The Heartland Institute, January 2013 (rev. May 2013), http://heartland.org/sites/default/files/05-15-13_common_core_revised_policy_brief_version.pdf.

7. See Herbert J. Walberg, *Tests, Testing, and Genuine School Reform* (Stanford, CA: Hoover Institution Education Next Press, 2011), pp. 78–80 for these and additional national survey results.

8. Christopher J. Klicka, "Decisions of the United States Supreme Court Upholding Parental Rights as 'Fundamental,'" Home Schooling Legal Defense Association, http://www.hslda.org/docs/nche/000000/00000075.asp, viewed June 9, 2013.

9. John E. Coons and Stephen D. Sugarman, *Education by Choice: The Case for Family Control* (1978, reprint, Troy, NY: Educator's International Press, Inc., 1999).

10. For this reason, Gary Becker referred to children as "durable consumption and production goods" in *The Economic Approach to Human Behavior* (Chicago, IL: University of Chicago Press, 1976).

11. Margaret Diane LeCompte and Anthony Gary Dworkin, *Giving Up on School: Student Dropouts and Teacher Burnouts* (Newbury Park, CA: Corwin Press, Inc., 1991), p. 83.

12. *Ibid.*, p. 84.

13. Herbert J. Walberg and Joseph L. Bast, "School Choice: The Essential Reform," *The Cato Journal* 13, no. 1 (Spring/Summer 1993): 101–21.

14. National Center for Education Statistics, "Back to School Statistics," http://nces.ed.gov/fastfacts/display.asp?id=372, viewed August 11, 2013.

15. Tom Loveless and Katharyn Field, "Perspectives on Charter Schools," Chapter 6 of Mark Berends, Matthew G. Springer, Dale Ballou, and Herbert J. Walberg, *Handbook of Research on School Choice* (New York, NY: Routledge, 2009), p. 101.

16. Richard Rothstein, "The Influence of Scholarship and Experience in Other Fields on Teacher Compensation Reform," in Matthew G. Springer, ed., *Performance Incentives: Their Growing Impact on American K–12 Education* (Washington, DC: Brookings Institution, 2009), pp. 87–109.

17. "Rules and Regulations," *Federal Register* 74, no. 221 (November 18, 2009): 59828–30, http://edocket.access.gpo.gov/2009/pdf/E9_27426.pdf.

18. *Ibid.*

19. *Ibid.*

20. Andy Smarick, "The Turnaround Fallacy," *Education Next*, Winter 2010, http://educationnext.org/the_turnaround_fallacy; David A. Stuit, "Are Bad Schools Immortal?" Thomas B. Fordham Institute, December 14, 2010, www.edexcellencemedia.net/publications/2010/20101214_AreBadSchoolImmortal/Fordham_Immortal.pdf.

21. Alyson Klein, "What's the Payoff for $4.6 Billion in School Improvement Grants?" *The Hechinger Report*, April 15, 2012.

22. Michael J. Mauboussin, "Blaming the Rat: Incentives, Motivation, and How They Interact," Legg Mason Capital Management, January 2011, http://www. lmcm. com/868298. pdf.

23. Friedrich A. Hayek, "The Use of Knowledge in Society," *American Economic Review* 35, no. 4 (September 1945): 519–30.

24. Clay Shirky, *Cognitive Surplus: Creativity and Generosity in a Connected Age* (New York, NY: Penguin Press, 2010).

25. Amy Chua, "China's Tigress Tycoons," *Newsweek*, March 5, 2012, http://www.thedailybeast.com/newsweek/2012/03/04/amy-chua-profiles-four-female-tycoons-in-china.html.

26. Alan Scher Zagier, "In South Korea, US Education Means Split Families," Associated Press, April 1, 2012, http://www.google.com/hostednews/ap/article/ALeqM5iZDny9ylD3ic5DR189L01UEAHjhA?docId=aa5ad9f346e246d49a99cc94460f8bf8.

27. Daniel H. Pink, *Drive: The Surprising Truth About What Motivates Us* (New York, NY: Riverhead Books, 2009).

28. Carol S. Dweck, *Mindset: The New Psychology of Success* (New York, NY: Random House, 2006).

29. John G. Nicholls, *The Competitive Ethos and Democratic Education* (Cambridge, MA: Harvard University Press, 1989).

30. Mario Weick and Ana Guinote, "How Long Will It Take? Power Biases Time Predictions," *Journal of Experimental Social Psychology* 46, no. 4 (July 2010): 595–604.

31. *Ibid.*

32. For example, see the Texas Education Code online at
http://www.statutes.legis.state.tx.us/?link=ED and a 2006 printed edition at
http://www.barnesandnoble.com/listing/2681386549284?r=1&cm_mmca2=pla&cm_mm
c=GooglePLA-_-Book_45Up-_-Q000000633-_-2681386549284.

33. Anon., "Catching On at Last: New Technology Is Poised to Disrupt America's
Schools, and Then the World's," *The Economist*, June 29, 2013,
http://www.economist.com/news/briefing/21580136-new-technology-poised-disrupt-ame
ricas-schools-and-then-worlds-catching-last.

PART TWO

How to Use Rewards

5

Rewards at Home

Rewards given to children by their parents, some of them given unknowingly, encourage learning everything from first words to the importance of deferred gratification and setting high but achievable goals. Appropriate use of rewards at home also helps create the grit or internal drive that supports lifelong learning and success.

Early Childhood Learning

Parents are children's first, most constant, and usually most important teachers. Parents can help their children remain focused even in the face of difficult, time-consuming tasks, a valuable trait for sustained success[1] and overcoming beliefs in inevitable failure.[2] These parental contributions can do much to help a child grow and mature psychologically.

Children learn to communicate with their parents well before they learn to talk, but to communicate well, children require more developed language skills. In a famous longitudinal study, Betty Hart and Todd Risley found parents' interactions with their children both inside and outside the home were strongly associated with their children's later IQ scores.[3] Children whose parents gave them more direct attention and involved them in frequent, high-quality conversations were more likely to develop stronger language skills over time. Similarly, households in which preschoolers regularly talked with their mothers, learned new vocabulary, were read to, and experienced nurturing, structured discipline were better prepared for school than preschoolers who did not experience such positive learning opportunities.[4]

Younger children especially benefit from concrete and immediate rewards for learning behavior. The earlier parents begin carefully planning goals and aligned rewards, the better for the child.[5] Parents can design meaningful goal-setting and learning habits with household routines and other activities such as family outings and vacations.

Parents may impose bans on playing outside or engaging in hobbies until the day's homework is done: These are everyday goals and aligned rewards. Some parents promise and plan entertaining activities such as a trip to the zoo or park in exchange for finishing homework or good grades in a child's most frustrating subject. Rewards can shape children's daily household activities as parents reinforce children's responsibility for their own learning, especially by encouraging leisure reading and other academically constructive activities.

Stanford economist Caroline Hoxby recalls that when she was young her mother rewarded her with caramels after daily piano practice. After she developed the self-discipline and music skills to enjoy playing for its own sake, Hoxby did not even notice she no longer needed the treat as an inducement to practice. Such acquired persistence pays off in other circumstances, including schooling. Angela Duckworth and Martin Seligman found that a student's level of self-discipline was twice as strong a predictor of school grades as IQ.[6]

Intentionally or not, parents set goals for themselves and their children. By imitating parents, children and adolescents learn how to plan meals, care for themselves, and manage their time. Parents who rely on authoritarian discipline expect their children to obey rules without question but deprive them of practice in setting goals. They may reward good behavior, but they prevent their child from helping to create cooperative family rules. On the other hand, excessively permissive parents offer too few guidelines and their children fall prey to minute-by-minute whims. "Moderate authoritative" rather than "authoritarian" parenting seems best, along with teaching children age-appropriate ways to set goals and to self-reward new learning as it unfolds.[7]

Eating habits are an early and obvious set of family routines that have long-lasting effects. When Sarah Anderson and Robert Whitaker looked at the relation between household routines and obesity among preschoolers living in the U.S., they found several useful guidelines for reducing child obesity.[8] Children who ate more than five family meals at home per week, slept at least 10.5 hours per night, and participated in fewer than two hours of screen-viewing activities per weekday were less likely than others to be obese. Adding even one of these routines seemed beneficial, but children whose families practiced all three were 63 percent less likely to be obese than those who did none. It is not clear what causes what; perhaps all of these are simply common indicators of healthy child rearing.

Parents' responses to their children's emotions teach children self-control. Rewards can be a key part of this process. Parents who employ a problem-solving approach to their children's emotional outbursts teach their children how to better control their emotions.[9] A parent might say, "Tell me why you are upset" in response to a child's screaming or crying, or "I see that you are angry because you wanted to play with that toy first. How can we make sure you get a turn? Should I set the timer for ten minutes for both of you?" Parents who respond emotionally to their children's outbursts can reinforce cycles of tension that tend to accelerate over time. Overly distant and overly controlling parents can limit a child's growth.[10] Finding humane, thoughtful ways to help children while at home helps them learn to care for themselves and succeed outside their homes.

Learning at Home

Nearly all children are "home schooled" during their first four or five years before being enrolled in a formal school. Growing numbers of students – approximately 1.7 million to 2.1 million[11] – continue to be schooled at home after they are old enough to attend conventional schools, but in some capacity all students continue to be, or should be, substantially "home schooled" for their entire K–12 careers. This is because in their first 18 years, only about 12 percent of children's time (when they're not sleeping) is spent in school.

Some parents do all they can to ensure their children rank first in all their academic classes in school. Best-selling author Amy Chua, for example, described herself as a "Tiger Mother" and was much ridiculed for her impressive and successful efforts to gain her daughters' entrance to Ivy League universities and for one to even make a solo performance at Carnegie Hall.[12] Her book, *Battle Hymn of the Tiger Mother*, noted that rigorous family emphasis on achievement is common in Asian cultures. It sparked a national debate about parents' roles in educating and pushing children to achieve.

Research shows children with devoted parents are likely to learn far more than others.[13] Parents can create a learning environment at home by having on hand age-appropriate personal or library-borrowed books and if they can afford it, art supplies, musical instruments, and electronic devices such as personal computers and tablets, which continue to fall in price. Many of these items can be purchased inexpensively at second-hand stores, such as Goodwill. Since children quickly outgrow many of these learning aids, it is a good idea to get in the habit of buying them used and then donating them when finished.

An extensive array of educational software is available from which parents can choose. Leaders in this field are Broderbund, creator of the Mavis Beacon typing software and Carmen Sandiego games, and Knowledge Adventure, with online and downloadable games in all fields for all age ranges.[14] The Core-Learning website offers a treasure trove of software and other resources for parents along with extensive reviews of education software.[15]

Excessive time spent watching television and playing video games is negatively associated with academic achievement, as well as positively correlated with child obesity, although the research is somewhat causally inconclusive.[16] While television may appear to be a free substitute for a babysitter, it can distract children as well as their parents from activities more likely to prompt learning and instill good habits such as playing board games, reading, painting, drawing, dancing, and participating in sports.

Activities that encourage learning should continue all the way through high school. Even though mom and dad may not be able to help much with chemistry, biology, and calculus homework, they can make sure there is a place for quiet study, that books and online resources are available, and that the usual preoccupations of young adults do not interfere with school work. At each stage of a child's development, age-appropriate rewards – from fruit or a trip to the park for infants to being able to use the car and staying out late on a weekend night for a teenager – are constructive parts of parenting. Reward systems need to be deliberately and carefully designed and then followed so that rewards are reliably given (or withheld) to help accelerate children's learning.

Homework

Once a child is enrolled in school, the time for homework starts. Sending children home from school with homework is a long tradition that has come under criticism by some psychologists and writers for being a form of punishment.[17] However, a recent review of research published from

1987–2003 conducted by a team of researchers from Duke University found "all studies, regardless of type, had design flaws, but there was generally consistent evidence for a positive influence of homework on achievement."[18] The strongest effect of homework on achievement occurred for students in grades 7-12.[19]

Students who learn to delay gratification while young are most likely to focus while they complete challenging homework assignments. All children and adolescents, however, can benefit from parent involvement in their homework. In a review of more than a dozen studies, such involvement resulted in higher rates of homework completion, fewer problems with assignments, and higher levels of achievement.[20]

Parents who thoughtfully encourage their children during homework reinforce the learners' persistence and nurture their evolving self-control. Such remarks might include "You can do it – it just takes hard work" or "Do not give up, you're almost finished."

Academic homework can be assigned by parents as well as by teachers. The Swann children – all ten of them – became renowned in the 1990s for graduating high school by the ages most students begin.[21] The oldest child in the family, Alexandra, emphasized she and her siblings were not geniuses. They just worked hard on a constant schedule. The family did not take summer vacation from school and their mother required them to understand all the material at hand before moving on. Alexandra and her sister Victoria earned bachelor's degrees at age 15 and master's degrees at age 16.

Though the Swanns' experiences are unusual, with access to new digital learning opportunities and greater flexibility of work hours and telecommuting, similar stories are becoming more common. Hard-working students may be ready to leave high school for college well before turning 17 or 18 and would gain little benefit from additional "seat time."[22]

After-School Activities

Parents can help their children choose stimulating after-school activities and build networks with other families to ensure their children spend their time constructively. Learners whose families help them identify suitable activities show higher levels of academic achievement than learners who do not participate in such activities.[23] Though many are not as rigorous as scientists would desire, studies across a wide range of programs and demographic groups show children in families with high-quality parent-child interaction, community support, and access to needed resources outside the school are more likely to become productive members of society.[24] One long-term study showed the Chicago Parent Centers, which combined child-rearing instruction with solidarity among parents, yielded favorable long-term results on school achievement and adult outcomes measured as late as age 26.[25]

Participating in constructive after-school activities, whether based at the school or hosted by other organizations such as churches and private clubs, creates new opportunities for children to learn from other children and adults. For parents it offers the opportunity to build bonds with other adults who can help them cope with the challenges of parenthood. Privately provided preschool and later out-of-school activities allow like-minded people such as those in various ethnic and religious groups to strengthen their shared interests. Children may benefit from the support of multiple adult caregivers and role models and from opportunities to gain recognition for their accomplishments and learning about their heritage. After-school activities in churches and private clubs – i.e., outside the regular school environment – provide children with a social group of their peers that is largely independent of their peers at their K–12 public school. For those who aren't fitting in well at school – especially in the middle-school years – these alternative peer groups may be particularly important.

After-school programs can be rich with opportunities for learning as well as effective use of rewards. Many programs recognize different levels of achievement and reward successful competitions with certificates, badges, and other forms of recognition for focused effort devoted to mastering a skill from reading poetry to learning to swim. Disciplined practice, which is so essential to mastery and advancement to higher levels of skill, may be easier in the presence of other students of similar skill levels who can help celebrate successes and commiserate over failures.

Parents can use enrollment in desirable programs as a reward for doing homework, high grades, or accomplishments in after-school programs. Other students or adults can be identified as role models simply by praising their efforts and achievements. Like other reward systems this must be accomplished without discouraging initial efforts or setting unrealistic goals. Goals should not be set too low, either: Students who graduate from high school with shelves filled with "participation trophies" without having demonstrated proficiency or a high level of skill may enter adulthood with inflated self-esteem and place unrealistic demands on colleges or employers for easy recognition and advancement. Success requires communicating with children about how and why goals are set and making the connection to rewards transparent.

As mentioned in the Introduction, participation in sports creates important opportunities for learning such skills as patience, persistence, teamwork, and goal-setting. Participation in sports also teaches the importance of practice to improve skill execution. The experience reported by Andrew Snow, a college student, that being part of a high-school basketball team was the experience that "best prepared me for college," is not at all uncommon.[26] Research finds sports as well as participation in clubs and organized activities produce beneficial effects on high-school graduation rates, college attendance, and civic responsibility, sometimes sufficient to overcome the negative effects of poverty and broken homes.[27] At least some of the positive effects of these activities can be traced to the positive feedback and rewards commonplace in such programs.

Sociologist James Coleman argued that strong relationships between parents and children within families, among parents within and across families, and between families and community organizations can provide a better environment for child-rearing and education.[28] He argued that solidarity among parents from different families could weaken the "adolescent society's" tendency toward school alienation and preference for entertainment, dating, and clothes over academic work. Stimulated by the work of economists, Coleman called the result of this social interaction "social capital."

As children grow older, their need for support from social capital becomes larger. Part-time and summer jobs were once a way for older children to connect with adults outside their own families, but this may be becoming less common. Laws requiring higher minimum wages and a record-slow recovery from the "Great Recession" of 2007–08 have made such jobs scarce. Meanwhile, more parents seem willing to give their children more than a token weekly "allowance," giving adolescents incomes without the need to find jobs. Economist Julian Simon said "it makes sense that in a time when jobs for school leavers are hard to come by, and while there is support available from the community and from the family, youths show the opposite of constructive effort – rebellion against the system, wanton attacks on persons and property, and self-destructive drug and alcohol abuse."[29] Of course, not all students react this way.

Rewards and the Culture of Poverty

If affluence creates perverse incentives for some children, a "culture of poverty" severely limits the opportunities other children have to benefit from structured play and enrollment in out-of-school programs.[30] This culture may include machismo, severely authoritarian decision-making, and disdain for education. The culture may accept resignation and passivity before life's challenges and even caregivers abandoning their children because of substance abuse. Some individuals living in a culture of poverty seem to live for the moment, ignoring the past and opportunities to plan for the future. Nevertheless, some children rise above such circumstances.[31] Connecting with other children and their families through after-school programs is often a constructive lifeline for these children.

Access to out-of-school resources is especially important for children from impoverished or broken homes.[32] Cultural and economic conditions limit parents' goal-setting and incentives for their children, whereas higher family income and wealth allow parents to provide better opportunities for their children – starting with where the family lives, which can be a determining factor in the quality of the schools, personal safety, and access to other community assets. Wealthier families can afford to send their children to private schools and pay for uniforms and equipment for sports teams. They may have multiple vehicles for transporting children back and forth from practices, rehearsals, and events, and perhaps a stay-at-home parent who can oversee the complicated schedule.

Nevertheless, middle-income and even poor families often can provide their children with similar but less-costly opportunities to learn outside school. One way is to utilize the extensive network of free or inexpensive clubs and facilities that often are nearby. YMCAs, YWCAs, Boy Scouts, Girl Scouts, Boys and Girls Clubs of America, park district or city-sponsored sports leagues, libraries, and programs provided by colleges and many private clubs are just some of the opportunities located in middle- and low-income communities.

"Surrogate parents" can extend social capital's lifeline to young people who otherwise would drift away. Asenath Andrews, principal of the Ferguson Academy for Young Women in Detroit, presides over a school that enrolls only pregnant unwed teen mothers very likely to drop out of school, yet the school graduates 95 percent of its students. The school admits young mothers, often born themselves to unwed mothers who dropped out of school, and attempts to break that cycle of poverty. It offers a full-day nursery for their children while the mothers study and attend class.

This environment – and Andrews' no-nonsense, motherly approach – enriches these young women's impoverished social capital by introducing them to words, ideas, and experiences far beyond their dingy apartments and streets.[33] "There are estimates that by age 3, poor kids have heard 30 million fewer words than kids in middle-class families," Andrews says. "That 30-million-word deficit keeps me awake at night. We're trying to teach teenagers to talk to their babies. Well, there's a whole vocabulary attached to a garden that these teenagers can share."

Overcoming Adversity

Children can learn to change how they react to difficult circumstances and increase their resilience to challenges.[34] A constantly negative outlook or feelings of powerlessness can be transformed into a positive, growth-oriented outlook if their circumstances are changed for the better. Children who are stuck in terrible homes and are currently unable to make sense of their circumstances still have the potential to acquire these coping skills later. According to Dante Cicchetti and John Curtis, research indicates such resilience is likely when children plan ahead, look to the future when setting goals, use active coping strategies, and directly confront their fears.[35]

Large-scale longitudinal studies have uncovered a number of ways people who experienced adversity in childhood became successful adults. Emmy E. Werner and Ruth S. Smith, for example, followed the entire birth cohort of children on the Hawaiian Island of Kauai for 40 years.[36] Among those who had one or more family risk factors such as mental illness, alcoholism, and drug addiction, one-third became caring, confident, employed adults. To use their language, the authors identified several "protective factors" leading to psychological "resilience" to family adversity. Two of the most consistent factors were a strong, enduring childhood bond with a caring, responsible non-parent caretaker such as a relative, babysitter, or teacher and regular activities with a religious or other charitable group.

With such adult supervision, children are more likely to receive material rewards, find friends, create supportive social relationships, and be exposed to cultural traditions that encourage a sense of heritage and resilience in the face of adversity. Given appropriate guidance, such social benefits strengthen a sense of purpose, a strong identity, and self-confidence. Think of the way many Native American tribes consciously teach their ancient rituals and tribal dances to young children and how many Orthodox Jewish children attend Hebrew school either full-time or every day after conventional school is over. Children also benefit from opportunities to care for themselves and others. They may feel a sense of unity as they engage in teamwork and build an optimistic view of the world when they see tangible results from their efforts. Even when children grow up in fractured households, they can thrive if they receive constructive outside support.

The ability to adapt to adverse and changing circumstances is an important life skill, and as these examples suggest, external as well as internal motivation play central roles in allowing learners to acquire such ability. Children with the problem-solving skills necessary to bounce back from adversity are more likely to remain constructively optimistic and to succeed despite trauma, a significant threat, or even prolonged adversity.

Resilience in the face of life's adversities allows children to prevail through difficulties, and these habits of mind can be cultivated. Rewards not only nurture resilience, they teach learners about the good they can accumulate when persistence and teamwork are aimed toward goals larger than themselves.

Conclusion

Parents assist their children's learning at home in a wide variety of ways that benefit from the judicious use of rewards. Parent-directed learning begins almost from the moment of birth as infants learn the basic skills of eating, washing hands, speaking, dressing themselves, and so on. Small and appropriate rewards for every step along the way are a natural and proper part of parenting, and research confirms these rewards are an effective way to teach life skills including self-discipline, deferred gratification, and perseverance.

As children grow older, parents can help their children learn by having their home well stocked with books, art supplies, musical instruments, and electronic and Internet-based educational devices. Avoiding non-educational television can be achieved by spending time on age-appropriate games, reading, and practice with painting, drawing, dancing, and sports.

When formal schooling begins, doing homework is often a child's first encounter with having to focus on and practice doing something that doesn't come from parents or isn't entertaining. It is an opportunity to measure progress and reward success while instilling good habits and teaching study skills. Making sure homework is completed on time and helping their children remain constructively engaged in school connects parents to schools and to educators who are entering the child's life for the first time. Parents well connected with parents in other families are likely to be more helpful to their children and others' children.

As the child grows older, in-school and out-of-school activities become more important and offer opportunities to measure and reward academic achievement, self-discipline, and good habits. By the time high school arrives the child may be acting out, an entirely rational response (as Julian Simon pointed out) to the incentives children face. Marshaling resources of "social capital" in the community can help children become aware of the opportunities that lie ahead – college or career choices – and understand the value of acquiring the knowledge and skills that will be necessary for a life of independence.

Children coming from poor or dysfunctional families face special challenges, but research suggests incentives and rewards are no less and perhaps even more important in helping them learn life skills. Poverty may rule out some out-of-school opportunities, but many opportunities valuable to the learning process are available to families regardless of their income. Resilient children who witness violence, alcoholism, and drug abuse at home can rise above adversity and learn skills that equip them for success later in life. At each step, rewards can play an important role: small, frequent, and concrete at first, and then gradually less frequent and more long-term (such as the promise of being able to enroll in a desirable college).

Parents should not be misled by popular writers into thinking rewards are inappropriate or counterproductive in the home learning environment. Experience and research show just the opposite: Home is where rewards can be most needed and most effective. Parents have a special responsibility to use rewards because professional educators often can't or won't extend their involvement outside the schools.

Notes

1. Lisa S. Blackwell, Kali H. Trzesniewski, and Carol Sorich Dweck, "Implicit Theories of Intelligence Predict Achievement Across Adolescent Transition: A Longitudinal Study and an Intervention," *Child Development* 78, no. 1 (January–February 2007): 246–63.

2. Catherine Good, Joshua Aronson, and Michael Inzlicht, "Improving Adolescents' Standardized Test Performance: An Intervention to Reduce the Effects of Stereotype Threat," *Applied Developmental Psychology* 24, no. 6 (December 2003): 645–62.

3. Betty Hart and Todd R. Risley, "American Parenting of Language-Learning Children: Persisting Differences in Family-Child Interactions Observed in Natural Home Environments," *Developmental Psychology* 28, no. 6 (November 1992): 1096–105.

4. Jeanne Brooks-Gunn and Lisa B. Markman, "The Contribution of Parenting to Ethnic and Racial Gaps in School Readiness," *The Future of Children* 15, no. 1 (Spring 2005): 139–68.

5. Rucker Johnson and Robert Schoeni, *The Influence of Early-Life Events on Human Capital, Health Status, and Labor Market Outcomes Over the Life Course* (Berkeley, CA: Institute for Research on Labor and Employment, 2006).

6. Angela L. Duckworth and Martin E.P. Seligman, "Self-Discipline Outdoes IQ in Predicting Academic Performance of Adolescents," *Psychological Science* 16, no. 12 (December 2005): 939–44.

7. Michael W. Pratt, Patricia Kerig, Philip A. Cowan, and Carolyn P. Cowan, "Mothers and Fathers Teaching 3-Year-Olds: Authoritative Parenting and Adult Scaffolding of Young Children's Learning," *Developmental Psychology* 24, no. 6 (November 1988): 832–9.

8. Sarah E. Anderson and Robert C. Whitaker, "Household Routines and Obesity in US Preschool-Aged Children," *Pediatrics* 125, no. 3 (March 2010): 420–8.

9. Nancy Eisenberg, Richard A. Fabes, Stephanie A. Shepard, Ivanna K. Guthrie, Bridget C. Murphy, and Mark Reiser, "Parental Reactions to Children's Negative Emotions: Longitudinal Relations to Quality of Children's Social Functioning," *Child Development* 70, no. 2 (March–April 1999): 513–34.

10. Wendy S. Grolnick and Richard M. Ryan, "Parent Styles Associated with Children's Self-Regulation and Competencies in School," *Journal of Educational Psychology* 81, no. 2 (June 1989): 143–54.

11. Home Schooling Legal Defense Association, http://www.hslda.org/research/faq.asp, viewed March 9, 2013.

12. Amy Chua, *Battle Hymn of the Tiger Mother* (New York, NY: The Penguin Press, 2011).

13. Arthur Reynolds and Suh-Ruu Ou, "Paths of Effects From Preschool to Adult Well-Being: A Confirmatory Analysis of the Child-Parent Center Program," *Child Development* 82, no. 2 (March–April 2011): 555–82.

14. See www.broderbund.com and www.knowledgeadventure.com, viewed March 13, 2013.

15. See www.corelearning.com; educational software reviews at http://www.core-learning.com/pt-ctr-reviews.asp, viewed March 13, 2013.

16. Anne Martin, David H. Saunders, Susan D. Shenkin, and John Sproule, "Lifestyle Intervention for Improving School Achievement in Overweight or Obese Children and Adolescents," Cochrane Developmental, Psychosocial and Learning Problems Group, March 14, 2012, DOI: 10.1002/14651858.CD009728; Tara Stevens, Lucy Barnard, and Yen M. To, "The Association Between Television Viewing and Achievement: The Impact of Optimal Viewing Across Time," *Teachers College Record*, January 26, 2009, http://www.tcrecord.org ID Number: 15498.

17. Alfie Kohn, *Feel-Bad Education and Other Contrarian Essays on Children and Schooling* (Boston, MA: Beacon Press, 2011), p. 61.

18. Harris Cooper, Jorgianne Civey Robinson, and Erika A. Patall, "Does Homework Improve Academic Achievement? A Synthesis of Research, 1987–2003," *Review of Educational Research* 76, no. 1 (Spring 2006): 1–62.

19. *Ibid.*

20. Erika A. Patall, Harris Cooper, and Jorgianne C. Robinson, "Parent Involvement in Homework: A Research Synthesis," *Review of Educational Research* 78, no. 4 (December 2008): 1039–101.

21. Alexandra Swann, *No Regrets* (Albuquerque, NM: Cygnet Press, 2010 [1989]).

22. Kathleen D. Noble, Sarah A. Childers, and Robert C. Vaughan, "A Place to Be Celebrated and Understood: The Impact of Early University Entrance From Parents' Points of View," *Gifted Child Quarterly* 52, no. 3 (Summer 2008): 256–68.

23. Harris Cooper, Jeffrey C. Valentine, Barbara Nye, and James J. Lindsay, "Relationships Between Five After-School Activities and Academic Achievement," *Journal of Educational Psychology* 91, no. 2 (June 1999): 369–78.

24. For a sample study involving twins, see Michel Duyme, Annick-Camille Dumaret, and Stanislaw Tomkiewicz, "How Can We Boost IQs of 'Dull Children'? A Late Adoption Study," *Proceedings of the National Academy of Sciences* 96, no. 15 (July 20, 1999): 8790–4.

25. Arthur J. Reynolds, Judy A. Temple, Barry White, Suu-Ruu Ou, and Dylan Robertson, "Age 26 Cost-Benefit Analysis of the Child-Parent Center Early Education Program," *Child Development* 82, no. 1 (January–February 2011): 379–404; Arthur J. Reynolds, Judy A. Temple, Dylan L. Robertson, and Emily A. Mann, "Long-Term Effects of an Early Childhood Intervention on Educational Achievement and Juvenile Arrest: A 15-Year Follow-up of Low-Income Children," *Journal of the American Medical Association* 285, no. 18 (May 9, 2001): 2339–46.

26. June Kronholz, "Academic Value of Non-Academics," *Education Next* 12, no. 1 (Winter 2012).

27. Michael J. Shanahan and Brian P. Flaherty, "Dynamic Patterns of Time Use in Adolescence," *Child Development* 72, no. 2 (March–April 2001): 385–401; Deborah Bobek, Jonathan Zaff, Yibing Li, and Richard M. Lerner, "Cognitive, Emotional, and Behavioral Components of Civic Action: Towards an Integrated Measure of Civic Engagement," *Journal of Applied Developmental Psychology* 30, no. 5 (September–October 2009): 615–27.

28. James S. Coleman, "Social Capital in the Creation of Human Capital," *American Journal of Sociology* 94, no. 1 (1988): S95–S120; and James S. Coleman, "Families and Schools," *Educational Researcher* 16, no. 6 (August–September 1987): 32–8.

29. Julian L. Simon, *Effort, Opportunity, and Wealth* (New York, NY: Basil Blackwell Ltd., 1987), p. 152.

30. See Oscar Lewis, "Culture of Poverty," in Daniel P. Moynihan, ed., *On Understanding Poverty: Perspectives from the Social Sciences* (New York, NY: Basic Books, 1969), pp. 187–220.

31. Jerome L. Singer, "Delay Gratification and Ego Development: Implications for Clinical and Experimental Research," *Journal of Consulting Psychology* 19, no. 4 (August 1955): 259–66.

32. Marian J. Bakermans-Krannenburg, Marinus H. van Ijzendoorn, and Robert H. Bradley, "Those Who Have, Receive: The Matthew Effect in Early Childhood Intervention in the Home Environment," *Review of Educational Research* 75, no. 1 (Spring 2005): 1–26.

33. Michele Owens, "Gardening to Save Detroit," *O Magazine*, April 2008, http://www.oprah.com/world/Gardening-in-the-City-Changing-Detroits-Landscape.

34. Richard J. Davidson and Sharon Bagley, *The Emotional Life of Your Brain* (New York, NY: Hudson Street Press, 2012).

35. Dante Cicchetti and W. John Curtis, "Multilevel Perspectives on Pathways to Resilient Functioning," *Development and Psychopathology* 19, no. 3 (Summer 2007): 627–9.

36. Emmy E. Werner and Ruth S. Smith, *Journey from Childhood to Midlife: Risk, Resilience, and Recovery* (Ithaca, NY: Cornell University Press, 2001).

6

Rewards in Elementary Schools

Parents may find themselves more involved than ever in their children's learning when a child enters elementary school, since working with teachers opens a door to a new level of activity. Parents and teachers can work together to plan and implement reward systems that are research-proven to help elementary-school children learn.

Home–School Collaboration

Children are more likely to thrive when parents and educators work together to increase students' achievement. Schools and community organizations have begun to recognize this and seek to engage parents actively in their children's educations. A foundation in Bridgeport, Connecticut recently began teaching parents "Civic Engagement 101," which focused on explaining how teacher evaluations work and what they convey about their children's teachers. In addition, the course outlines strategies for parents to get teachers and schools to consider what individual parents believe is best for their children in the classroom.[1]

In only two years, an initiative in Detroit aimed at promoting parent involvement to help the long-troubled school district met notable success. Contracting with Detroit Public Schools, the Detroit Parent Network increased parent involvement in schools by 37 percent in its first year. The initiative offers parenting workshops and information about food, health care, schools, and education.[2]

Findings from studies using a wide range of methods and designs confirm the value of parent involvement in their children's school activities.

A synthesis (meta-analysis) of 52 studies conducted in urban schools found students whose parents were involved in their children's education showed notably greater levels of achievement than students whose parents were not.[3] In one study, home-schooled and schooled children who reported the highest level of parental involvement in their educations also showed the highest levels of achievement.[4] Children of parents who set high expectations for them also performed well in school.

A useful list of ways parents can work with elementary schools appears on the website of the U.S. Department of Education. It includes tips shown in the table on the following page.

Parents in Classrooms

Parents becoming directly involved in their children's classrooms often create readily apparent benefits. One review of 14 studies that included more than 1,000 families found children made marked gains in reading and writing when their parents helped in classrooms, some even teaching specific skills.[5] In other research, benefits from parental involvement in the classroom appeared to depend on the parents' enthusiasm.[6]

Parents seem increasingly to understand this and deliberately participate in their children's education because of it. The 28th (2012) survey by Harris Interactive of teachers, students, and parents shows parent engagement levels are among the highest they have ever been.[7] Forty-eight percent of students report their parents visit school once a month, a number almost three times greater than in 1988 when the survey was first taken (16 percent). Two-thirds of students say they talk about school with their parents every day, more than four times as many as did when the survey was first taken. And teachers with greater levels of parent involvement in their classes report much higher job satisfaction.

Of course, parents can become too involved in their children's education. Learners' intellectual development suffers when parents' attention undermines their self-confidence. In one 18-month longitudinal study, Eva Pomerantz and Missa Murry Eaton found some mothers became overly intrusive because they worried excessively about their children's achievement or because children exhibited high levels of uncertainty.[8]

Intrusive mothers were more likely to monitor their children's progress or offer to do things for their children when the children did not ask for such help. These mothers considered their intrusive actions essential for their children's success. Unfortunately, despite these parents' good

Ways Parents Can Work with Elementary Schools

- Visit a classroom in the school.
- Get a copy of the school's parent involvement plan.
- Volunteer to be a room parent, organize a winter coat drive, help out on test day, or be a reading coach.
- Ask the principal for the school's report card.
- Find out the best time to contact educators by telephone.
- Ask for the teacher's e-mail address.
- Find out about websites where teachers may list class notes and homework assignments.
- Participate in parent-teacher conferences.
- Be prepared to listen, talk, and take notes.
- Write out questions before meeting with the teacher.
- Ask for specific information about the child's work and progress.
- Review what the teacher suggested and follow up by talking with the child.
- Check back with the teacher regularly to see how things are going as the year progresses.
- Know that counselors can help if there are problems at home, such as divorce or illness.

Source: U.S. Department of Education, "Parent Power: Build the Bridge to Success," http://www2.ed.gov/parents/academic/help/parentpower/booklet.pdf, last visited March 10, 2013. See the source for original phrasing of these points.

intentions, intrusiveness did not spark greater levels of achievement. Finding a balance between offering assistance and encouragement and allowing independence may take time and calls for parents' and educators' wisdom.

Planning Classroom Reward Systems

When planning classroom reward systems, educators have to consider and balance multiple perspectives including compliance with federal, local school district, and individual school guidelines and the wishes of principals, parents, and students. As in other decision-making,[9] teachers consider the learner's abilities as they identify tasks to accomplish and the problems associated with each task. Teachers specify learning goals and the best methods for achieving each one.[10]

Teachers design lesson activities and imagine the consequences of using each one before implementing it, keeping in mind the specific children in their classes. Such planning allows teachers to align rewards with curricular goals. Research has found the lack of sufficient planning is a major cause of disciplinary problems and other disruptions of classroom learning, which may be attributable to lessons too difficult, too easy, or otherwise unrewarding.[11]

Teachers are expected to clarify matters that are confusing, evaluate each activity, and consider how well lessons from one day best fit with lessons from other days. Repeating lessons can be as boring for teachers as it is for students but as noted earlier, some forms of repetition are beneficial. Nevertheless, too much repetition of material already learned may try learners' patience. Even very small rewards can help young learners cope with this challenge and can readily be adapted to differences in what individual learners already know and how fast they can learn new material.

It is easy for teachers to miss many of the ways they create incentives in their usual classroom routines. Young children like to show what they know to those who will listen sympathetically and sincerely. They may require rewards such as listening and gold stars that can be easily given and readily understood. Insightful, skillful teachers instinctively consider and act on their students' likely reactions to incentives. They notice what does and does not constitute a reward for a particular child or group of children.

Praise

Some critics of rewards – Alfie Kohn, for example – even criticize the use of praise in classrooms.[12] Their rationale is that the selective use of praise constitutes the assertion of "power" by an adult over children and that too much praise dilutes its value. As we've observed before, praise can be undeserved or poorly timed, resulting in an inflated sense of self-esteem. This kind of reward may in fact be overused today by many parents and educators. But this misuse of rewards means teachers and parents need better advice on how to use praise more judiciously, not that they shouldn't use it at all.

Interviews with elementary students in grades 1 through 5 showed children are astute recipients of classroom rewards and value the rewards that best help them improve their learning.[13] Research shows offering students detailed feedback and emphasizing their effort raises the motivation of most students, especially those with learning disabilities.[14] Children who receive encouragement that outlines something they did well and something to improve on do better than students who are told vaguely that they are "good students" or are "smart."[15]

Children can be such astute observers that they see subtle cues about what answers parents and teachers expect, which leads them to appear skilled when they are merely imitating others or even guessing good answers from teachers' facial expressions as they drift closer to the desirable answer – all without understanding the reasoning behind the right answer. This is a tactic teachers need to recognize and try to counter.

Rewards Built Into Activities

Many rewards in elementary school classrooms arise from the learning process itself. Young children experience pleasure when discovering new information or developing a new skill. In an elementary school classroom this should be occurring with great frequency. Teachers should be on the lookout for small as well as big achievements, should congratulate young learners, and when appropriate, should point out how even small achievements will make further achievements easier.

Very young children experience pleasure when they are able to recognize and pronounce the names of simple objects, such as fruits or animals. Direct Instruction authority Siegfried Engelmann uses this principle in teaching reading.[16] When reading a short story the first time, the teacher covers the illustration for the words he or she reads, both to keep it a surprise and to prevent the child from guessing at the words by looking at the picture. After the child has sounded out the words phonetically, the teacher uncovers the picture, rewarding the child for decoding the words that describe it. In this instance, both pronouncing the correct sounds and viewing the corresponding picture reward the child for his or her accomplishment.

As children grow older and objects become more familiar, they may enjoy finding objects hidden in larger pictures, then coloring pictures of familiar objects, and then being able to draw pictures themselves. Using art as a learning activity, described below, is an example of a learning activity with rewards "built in."

Stickers, Parties, and Prizes

Though disparaged by Alfie Kohn, stickers, prizes, and parties can be appropriately used in preschool and elementary classrooms. Without these tangible rewards or feedback from their teachers, students may be unsure if they performed a task successfully or of the value of the task they performed, or they may quickly forget it. Rewards convey valuable information to even the youngest learner and make learning specific knowledge and insights memorable, an essential step toward further learning.

Elementary school teachers do this, for example, when awarding small children construction paper "ice cream scoops" for each multiplication set they memorize or book they read outside of class. Nearly all children like ice cream, so the appearance of another scoop in their cone is immediately understood as a good thing whereas a longer row of stars or a higher grade may not convey that understanding as quickly or as clearly.[17] All the children can see whose "ice cream cone" is largest and most will readily compete for it to be theirs. This symbolic reward has the added advantage of having no sugar.

Other rewards may be as simple as a sticker attached to a paper or one that can be worn on a shirt or jacket, or designating a child "teacher's helper for the week." Parties and prizes celebrating individual or group successes, such as perfect attendance or completion of a multi-step project, amount to a combination of small rewards – surprise, entertainment, success in a competition, and recognition – that make an achievement especially memorable.

It is a testament to the success of such systems that receiving rewards is often the first thing reported by elementary students, often with great pride and excitement, when they see a parent after school. By making achievement memorable, these small rewards make a big difference.

Grades

Another valuable but often-criticized form of reward is grades.[18] Students are eager to know "how I did" on a project or a test. The desire is entirely natural and correct: Part of maturing is subjecting our accomplishments to the judgment of other people, and having papers, tests, artwork, and other activities graded is a consistent way of doing this. Whether grades in every case should be made public is a different matter. A case can be made that consistently low grades can de-motivate and shame young learners, reducing their motivation to do better.

It is often advantageous to let students know how tests and other activities will count on their grades and the numerical criteria for various grades. The lazy way to do this is to "grade on the curve"; that is, to give grades based on the percentages of students who attain various test scores, homework grades, and other indicators. The research does not give a strong indication of whether this method is better than a straight grading scale assigning letter grades for certain percentages of correct answers, but it is unconstructive, if not wrong, to give high grades for substandard work. Like praise lavished on students for mediocre accomplishment, grade inflation can mislead students into thinking they have achieved proficiency or mastery when they have not. This may create happy students and parents but it does not promote and may actually retard learning.

The movement away from grading students' work has been widespread because of concerns, similar to those expressed about praise, that they represent an improper or unnecessary expression of adult power or authority in classrooms. The foundation of this concern seems more ideological than pedagogical, and the influence of the movement on student achievement seems to be mostly negative.[19] While grading of all sorts is more prevalent in higher grades, it is appropriate in elementary schools, keeping in mind the caveats already expressed.

Art, Music, and Drama

Art, as mentioned previously, offers a rich arena for elementary student learning in which rewards are already built in. Because of the limits of their vocabulary and experience, younger students often have difficulty expressing their ideas. Art can encourage children to develop their communication skills.[20] Their drawings and pictures may help them translate their experience and knowledge into images and then into words.

Children benefit from opportunities to express their emotions with music. Singing, playing instruments, and responding to music provide valuable opportunities and incentives to express emotions. This is the basis for Kindermusik, a popular set of programs for young children that teaches them rhythm, rhyming, balance, and other important musical and social abilities.[21] Children as young as newborns listen to age-appropriate sounds and songs and learn to tap thick dowels to a beat, dance and stretch with colorful scarves, sing nursery rhymes, and shake maracas.

Drama teaches children more skills than may seem obvious from the resulting presentation. Children can learn to plan, represent ideas in a script, and imagine other people's perspectives. They learn to develop their memories and, when acting out famous historical scenes or plays, join a tradition of communication and ideas. Since a single error by a director, stagehand, or actor can greatly diminish the power of a production, they can discover the importance of all members playing their parts well.

Art, music, and drama help children not only to express themselves but to appreciate the ways people communicate. They can learn much both by appreciation and direct participation.

Paying for Achievement

Surprising though it may seem, children as early as second-grade can be motivated to learn by the promise of money, whether real or "play," that can be used to purchase school supplies or other goods and services. The use of such reward systems is not new and it appears to be fairly extensive, at least in private schools.[22]

The rationale for offering money to elementary students is straightforward. Children from their earliest ages see money being used to pay for goods and services and naturally desire to imitate the behavior of adults and older children who have solved the riddle of exchanging a token for a desired item. Handling money, whether real or play, teaches math skills, the value of deferred gratification, and (at least in higher grades) economic lessons. To the degree that learning can be difficult – and we readily concede it not always is and shouldn't be presented this way to younger students – students understand intuitively the fairness of the transaction: They are paid for working hard. Finally, real money and to a lesser extent play money can be used to buy a variety of items that may be desired by students, making it more likely to motivate more students than, say, offering pencils or books.

A controlled study involving second-graders in Texas paid $2 for each grade-appropriate book they read outside of class – a simple assignment and a modest reward to accomplish it.[23] The students could earn up to $40, though the average earnings were $13. Eighty percent of the learners offered this reward read at least one book for pay, and all those who participated improved their reading comprehension.

Rewards for Healthy Eating

A seemingly unending struggle for educators and parents is getting children to resist their craving for vitamin-empty sugars and starches, which often leads to sacrificing healthy foods and risks common obesity. Two economists, David Just and Joseph Price, reported[24] that a federal regulation impelled the nation's schools to serve an extra $5.4 million worth of fruits and vegetables each school day, of which $3.4 million went uneaten.

To identify promising solutions, Just and Price carried out a week-long experiment in 15 public elementary schools. They paid more than 9,000 students in several separate groups a nickel, a quarter, or a raffle ticket for a larger amount for eating each vegetable or fruit serving. On average, the rewards resulted in an 80 percent increase in these servings over baseline amounts.

After the week's experiment, however, students resumed their less healthy consumption patterns, and the two economists are investigating rewards over longer periods and the possibility of lasting changes in habits. Given students' poor dietary habits, continued payments even without habituation might be worthwhile. Presumably, moreover, monetary and other rewards for healthy eating at home might be similarly worthwhile. Given the consistency of reward effects illustrated in this book, more lasting effects might be expected.

Student-Initiated Rewards

Elementary students can be given some authority over classroom policies and activities. Lesson plans are rarely so tightly scripted that some of the preferences expressed by children cannot be incorporated into daily activities. Allowing them to choose from a range of serious options may strengthen their commitment to assigned tasks.[25]

Many children appreciate the opportunity to make and then see the consequences of choices that involve themselves as well as others. Participating in classroom management is an opportunity to learn listening, teamwork, and negotiating skills. The increase in social status that comes from being part of a team that decides the destination of a field trip, for example, can be large for a seven- or eight-year-old and thus creates a major incentive to focus on doing the job well.

This sort of flexibility resulted in a group of students in Washington state becoming instrumental in naming the state crustacean in 2009 when their fourth-grade teacher, Stephanie Buzbee, encouraged them to study differences among states.[26] One child discovered that Louisiana had a state crustacean but Washington did not. Her father, a state lawmaker, called Buzbee to talk about it. She told her students to research whether naming a state crustacean was a good idea and why. They did, and later took their research to the state legislature after preparing and practicing speeches to deliver to lawmakers.

Elementary teachers can include their students in discussions of classroom management and other matters without sliding into Rousseauian permissiveness, but erring in that direction seems all too common. For example, a sixth grade social studies teacher in Illinois announced on his blog in 2011 that "I now see the futility of teaching my students. I have found that telling my students what to do does not make them learn. ... So, I am giving it all up. I am done teaching my students. I will no longer give pencil and paper tests. I refuse to tell my students what projects to do." This teacher then declared his goal is to "become invisible and the students will take complete control over their learning."[27] A year after posting this statement, the teacher was named Illinois' "2012 Teacher of the Year."

A *New Yorker* cartoon from several decades ago showed a boy with raised hand asking, "Do we have to do what we want to do today?" It's a question that needs to be asked in too many classrooms. Children often recognize the value of structure and guidance even when the adults around them have been persuaded otherwise.

Conclusion

Well-designed and carefully implemented reward systems can improve student achievement in elementary schools. While young children are often intrinsically motivated, they benefit when their accomplishments, however small, are pointed out by parents and teachers and appropriately rewarded. Not all learning is easy or entertaining, and the presence of incentives and rewards can help young learners confront and overcome obstacles and distractions.

Parents are their children's most important and effective teachers. They should be using rewards at home before their children enter school and they should continue to use them through their children's entire K–12 careers. They should express their concerns to teachers and principals if it appears rewards are not being correctly used in their children's classrooms, perhaps by using some of the dozen different ways they can work with their schools described by the U.S. Department of Education booklet summarized on page 79.

At least seven kinds of rewards are appropriate and effective in elementary schools: verbal praise, rewards built into lessons, small tokens (stickers, parties, and prizes), grades, arts incentives, money (real or play), and student-initiated rewards.

The use of these forms of incentives and rewards with children and adults is not due to some mass delusion about their effectiveness nor some insidious plot to condition people for lives as workers for some elite. The incentives are used because parents, teachers, and students themselves recognize that they work and appreciate them. Teachers should not be afraid to use them more often and parents should not hesitate to challenge teachers and administrators if such rewards seem to be absent from their children's schools.

Notes

1. Michele Molnar, "Bridgeport Community Association to Teach Parents Advocacy," *Education Week*, March 6, 2012,
http://blogs.edweek.org/edweek/parentsandthepublic/2012/03/
bridgeport-community-association-to-teach-parents-advocacy.html.

2. Joy Pullmann, "DPS Reform a Model for the City," *Detroit News*, January 10, 2012.

3. William H. Jeynes, "The Relationship Between Parental Involvement and Urban Secondary School Student Academic Achievement: A Meta-Analysis," *Urban Education* 42, no. 1 (January 2007): 82–110. Note achievement comparisons of students with and without parental involvement showed differences that were . 5 to . 55 of a standard deviation, regardless of how achievement was defined.

4. Laura M. Barwegen, Nancy K. Falciani, S. Junlah Putnam, Megan B. Reamer, and Esther E. Stair, "Academic Achievement of Homeschool and Public School Students and Student Perception of Parent Involvement," *The School Community Journal* 14, no. 1 (Spring/Summer 2004): 39–58.

5. Monique Sénéchal, *The Effect of Family Literacy Interventions on Children's Acquisition of Reading from Kindergarten to Grade 3: A Meta-Analytic Review* (Portsmouth, NH: RMC Research Corporation, 2006).

6. Gail L. Zellman and Jill M. Waterman, "Understanding the Impact of Parent School Involvement on Children's Educational Outcomes," *The Journal of Educational Research* 91, no. 6 (1998): 370–80.

7. Metlife Survey of the American Teacher, March 2012,
http://www.metlife.com/assets/cao/contributions/foundation/american-teacher/MetLife-T
eacher-Survey-2011.pdf.

8. Eva Pomerantz and Missa Murry Eaton, "Maternal Intrusive Support in the Academic Context: Transactional Socialization Processes," *Developmental Psychology* 37, no. 2 (March 2001): 174–86.

9. John S. Hammond, Ralph L. Keeney, and Howard Raiffa, *Smart Choices: A Practical Guide to Making Better Decisions* (Boston, MA: Harvard Business School Press, 1999).

10. As in equally complicated industries, many of these determinations and decisions could be done once and well, and educators could concentrate on teaching rather than deciding what to teach. Technology can contribute by relieving them of minute-by-minute assessing of individual students' progress. We will discuss this at length in Part 3.

11. Dennis G. Wiseman and Gilbert H. Hunt, *Best Practice in Motivation and Management in the Classroom* (Springfield, IL: Charles C. Thomas Publisher Ltd., 2008).

12. Alfie Kohn, *Punished by Rewards: The Trouble with Gold Stars, Incentive Plans, A's, Praise, and Other Bribes* (New York, NY: Houghton Mifflin, 1993), pp. 96ff.

13. Theresa A. Thorkildsen, Susan Bobbit Nolen, and Janice Fournier, "What's Fair? Children's Critiques of Practices that Influence Motivation," *Journal of Educational Psychology* 86, no. 4 (December 1994): 475–86.

14. Dale H. Schunk, "Effects of Effort Attributional Feedback on Children's Perceived Self-Efficacy and Achievement," *Journal of Educational Psychology* 74, no. 4 (August 1982): 548–56; and Dale H. Schunk and Paula D. Cox, "Strategy Training and Attributional Feedback with Learning Disabled Students," *Journal of Educational Psychology* 78, no. 3 (June 1986): 201–9.

15. Avraham N. Kluger and Angelo DeNisi, "The Effects of Feedback Interventions on Performance: A Historical Review, a Meta-Analysis, and a Preliminary Feedback Intervention Theory," *Psychological Bulletin* 119, no. 2 (March 1996): 254–84.

16. As described by Shepard Barbash, *Clear Teaching* (Arlington, VA: Education Consumers Foundation, 2012).

17. For an example, see http://www.uniqueteachingresources.com/multiplication-sticker-charts.html, viewed March 19, 2013.

18. Alfie Kohn, *supra* note 12, pp. 200ff.

19. Jeanne S. Chall, *The Academic Achievement Challenge: What Really Works in the Classroom?* (New York, NY: The Guilford Press, 2000); E.D. Hirsch, Jr., *The Schools We Need and Why We Don't Have Them* (New York, NY: Doubleday, 1996); Victor Davis Hanson and John Heath, *Who Killed Homer? The Decline of Classical Education and the Recovery of Greek Wisdom* (New York, NY: The Free Press, 1998).

20. Rob Barnes, *Teaching Art to Young Children 4–9*, 2nd ed. (New York, NY: Routledge-Falmer, 2002).

21. See http://www.kindermusik.com/, viewed on March 10, 2013.

22. Dewey Lipe and Steven M. Jung, "Manipulating Incentives to Enhance School Learning," *Review of Educational Research* 41, no. 4 (October 1971).

23. Bradley Allen and Roland Fryer Jr., "The Power and Pitfalls of Education Incentives," *Discussion Paper 2011-07*, The Hamilton Project, September 2011, http://www.brookings.edu/research/papers/2011/09/incentives-fryer-allen.

24. David R. Just and Joseph Price, "Using Incentives to Encourage Healthy Eating in Children," *Journal of Human Resources* 48, no. 4 (2013): 855–72.

25. Wendy S. Grolnick and Richard M. Ryan, "Autonomy in Children's Learning: An Experimental and Individual Difference Investigation," *Journal of Personality and Social Psychology* 52, no. 5 (May 1987): 890–8.

26. Ryan Cost, "After a Simple Question, Fourth Graders Find Themselves Becoming Citizen Lobbyists," *The Oregonian*, January 28, 2012, http://www.oregonlive.com/politics/index.ssf/2012/01/fourth-graders-find-success-as.html.

27. Josh Stumpenhorst, "I Resign from Teaching," http://stumpteacher.blogspot.com/2011/02/i-resign-from-teaching.html, viewed August 9, 2013.

7

Rewards in Secondary Schools

Adults can support adolescents' learning by helping them define goals, by suggesting learning strategies, by creating positive incentives, and by delivering aligned rewards.[1] Economic and psychological research makes clear that reward systems can significantly raise academic achievement levels and high-school graduation rates for adolescents.

A review of the literature reveals many reward systems that have successfully motivated adolescents to stay in school and remain focused on academic achievement. Some of these techniques were described in previous chapters and need only be adapted to middle- and high-school classrooms, while others involving tests and digital learning will be described in Part 3. The remaining reward systems fall into four categories: successful classroom techniques, paying for achievement, strategies for self-teaching, and incentives for non-college-bound students to graduate.

Classroom Techniques

Interest in school often declines in adolescence,[2] perhaps due to the incentives described earlier by Simon, the influence of "adolescent culture" described earlier by Coleman, or the confluence of adolescent hormones and popular culture that parents cannot fail to notice. This decline in academic interest sometimes leads students into self-destructive behavior.[3] Schools can help counter this tendency with a variety of classroom techniques that reward students who stay focused on their studies.

Schools can use some of the reward systems we described in the previous chapter while recognizing that students' human and social capital grows as they acquire knowledge, skills, personal possessions, and reputation. Since the power of incentives to prompt effort depends on their size relative to students' current capital, rewards may need to change.[4] Older children and adolescents are more likely than elementary students to appreciate less-tangible rewards such as honor and attention from people they admire; expressions of trust, such as being able to use the family car or stay out later than normal for special occasions; and longer-term rewards, such as passing Advanced Placement exams and admission to elite universities of their choice. Older children are more sensitive to having input into their learning goals and are inclined to resist incentives they perceive to be exercises of arbitrary authority by adults.

Pam Grossman and her colleagues identified eight features of instruction that create positive incentives for achievement by middle-school students. They are listed in the table on the following page.[5]

These techniques underscore how using rewards in classrooms isn't restricted to "carrots and sticks" that may or may not reflect the wants and abilities of students. Instead, many of these techniques involve getting students to share with teachers what their real interests and goals are and thereby revealing the best ways to motivate them. The best reward systems require discovering students' motivations, not assuming them.[6]

Paying for Achievement

Access to money, even play money, becomes increasingly important as students get older and discover that meeting many of their wants requires having money. Part-time jobs begin to compete with school and homework as students enter middle- and high-school, making pay for academic achievement one way to fight back. However, this is not the only way and can fail to produce the desired results unless done carefully.

A particularly intriguing example of paying middle-school students is the Knowledge Is Power Program (KIPP), a nationwide group of open-enrollment college preparatory schools commonly located in urban and poor communities.[7] These schools rely heavily on financial and non-financial rewards to motivate students who might not otherwise experience a rigorous education. KIPP students typically receive 60 percent more instruction than students at other schools attributable to a longer school day, mandatory summer school, and a wide range of after-school activities. Keeping students focused can be a special challenge.

Effective Classroom Techniques for Adolescents

- Describe the purpose of each educational activity, giving students reasons to want to do it rather than just being told to obey instructions from an authority figure.

- Promote activities as intellectual challenges, lifting them above just another chapter or assignment to an opportunity for discovery, mastery, or a way to make future activities easier.

- Explain key concepts in several different ways, recognizing that by middle school students' bases of knowledge and skills have evolved differently, resulting in different abilities to grasp concepts based on how they are presented.

- Connect new information to prior knowledge or personal preferences, showing that acquiring the new information fits into and increases a student's store of knowledge and therefore his or her "wealth."

- Use their own behavior as a model, since adolescents are highly attuned to evidence of hypocrisy by adults and increasingly want to be viewed as grown-ups.

- Include guided and deliberate practice in order to achieve automaticity and stored memory.

- Provide clear and detailed feedback so students know what is expected of them and when they have performed well so they are persuaded that a grade or disciplinary action is fair.

- Generate classroom discussion since shyness or defeatism can discourage adolescents from speaking directly to an adult teacher or being first to ask a question during class.

Source: Pam Grossman, Susanna Loeb, Julia Cohen, Karen Hammerness, James Wyckoff, Donald Boyd, and Hamilton Lankford, "Measure for Measure: The Relationship Between Measures of Instructional Practice in Middle School English Language Arts and Teachers' Value-Added Scores," *Working Paper 16015*, National Bureau of Economic Research, 2010. See the source for original phrasing of these points.

At the end of each week, each middle-school student receives a paycheck in "KIPP dollars" to reward effort, good behavior, and completed homework. KIPP dollars are not real dollars, can be used only within KIPP schools, and are used exclusively to reward effort and not for getting good grades or passing tests. Students' pay may be "debited" for misbehaving. The paychecks can be used to purchase notebooks, writing supplies, snacks, and more from a school store as well as the right to participate in field trips to such places as Washington, DC and the Grand Canyon.

According to one report on the reward system, "The Paycheck Program has achieved its primary goal, improving student behavior and communication between students and faculty. When the principal hands out the paychecks on Friday afternoon, positive conversations usually result. Reinforcement of the students' behaviors makes them think about consequences and better understand expectations, the staff members have said. Communication with parents has been amplified as well. Weekly feedback on a child's behavior prompts regular dialogue between parents and teachers."[8]

In an interview with PBS, KIPP co-founder Mike Feinberg explained why the schools use rewards and incentives. "Well, it goes back to the general premise that ... when you do the right thing, good things happen and when you do the wrong thing, bad things happen. I know it doesn't always work out that way in life but it usually follows that pattern and we want the kids to learn that valuable life lesson," Feinberg said.[9] He continued:

[C]hildren who are at public schools ... don't feel the sense of earning things which we know exists beyond education out there in the real world. They're entitled to their desk, they're entitled to books, they're entitled to the breakfast and the lunch, they're entitled to have a teacher in front of them, they're entitled to be in a school building that's somewhere in their neighborhood. ... [W]ithout teaching the value that things need to get earned, you can create a situation where kids grow up thinking that this is going to keep happening, that they're going to be entitled to a college education, they're going to be entitled to become a lawyer, doctor, architect, engineer, whatever they want to do in this world.[10]

Strategies for Self-Teaching

When asked to determine the best ways to learn science, adolescents said they would learn more if teachers explained and showed the means of scientific inquiry and then let students try to conduct their own tests of theories.[11] Their interest in "self-teaching" is consistent with the economic theory of incentives since rewards can be smaller but still motivating if an effective strategy of learning lowers the cost (in time and effort) of acquiring something of value. Such self-monitoring and error correction will be quicker and more frequent than what a teacher, even a tutor, can provide.

Grossman and her colleagues, the source of the classroom techniques listed above, found students given explicit instructions on strategies for learning were most likely to experience boosts in achievement. The highest achievement levels were found among students whose teachers showed them how to plan their studying, monitor their own progress, and efficiently retrieve information that would be valuable for reviewing before tests or when tackling the next and higher level of learning.

Courses designed to teach young people the attitudes and habits necessary for high achievement include Brainology,[12] a set of classes for middle-school students developed by *Mindset* author and Stanford psychology professor Carol Dweck. The courses teach young people neuroscience focused on how their brains work and respond to certain study techniques, then outline and reinforce the study techniques themselves. Brainology is a blended learning class in which part of the instruction is conducted online through videos and interactive exercises and part is conducted in the classroom with a teacher and fellow students.

The popularity of robotic science programs such as Lego Mindstorms[13] illustrates the appeal of self-teaching. Students use kits containing gears, wheels, "servo motors with built-in rotation sensors," and other components to build robots. Schools and community organizations field Lego robotics teams that compete to see which team or individual can most quickly create a robot that can solve a particular challenge or set of challenges, such as navigating an obstacle course or swimming towards an underwater target.

Growing access to personal computers and the Internet is a boon for self-teaching. Several computer programs, for example, detect spelling and grammar errors. Regular use of these programs provides consistent and repetitive feedback to students to solidify correct writing practices. Students also can find and sign up for free online courses from organizations such as

Khan Academy[14] and circulate their work for comment and correction to teachers, students, and even newspaper editors and academics.

Teachers may recognize technology is transforming schooling but may not see how it is enabling a style of learning that rewards students who remain focused on academics. Students need to be steered away from mindless video games and other distractions and toward sites that help them accelerate their ability to learn new things, thereby making their time in school more likely to lead to graduation, post-secondary schooling, and a desired occupation. Chapter 10 addresses some of these new learning technologies in detail.

Incentives for Non-College-Bound Students

Chapter 3 summarized research showing the powerful effects of paying high-school students to pass Advanced Placement exams and providing college tuition for students who do well on rigorous curriculum-based examinations. But what about non-college-bound students who may be interested in working as soon as possible, some even before graduation? They may be sorely frustrated with their academic high-school experience. Their frustration can help explain dropout rates of 50 percent or higher in many big-city public high schools. Some dropouts may return to school later or pursue General Educational Development (GED) diplomas that require passing tests rather than regularly attending conventional high schools, but this may be a poor substitute for a regular diploma.[15]

Most Asian and European school systems assume some students will end their school careers after nine years, the end of "lower secondary school," to use the international term. Only college-bound students are expected to go on for three more years of upper secondary education before college. Some systems have two types of schools corresponding to student abilities and interests: the academic, featuring abstract and advanced work for the college-bound, and the vocational, featuring job knowledge and skills tracks for those working towards technical occupations, some highly paid such as optometry.

In the U.S., the widespread assumption among educators and policymakers is that every student should graduate "college ready" and immediately advance to college. This assumption is noble, as it shows high expectations and the traditional American faith in egalitarianism. But slower students may deter the progress of other students. Many students who pursue four-year college degrees never finish and receive little if any return on their investments of time and money for tuition. In fact, many are worse off since they are saddled with student debt.[16] Those who graduate from inferior institutions and programs may not recover through higher wages the full cost of their college education, particularly given a four-year or longer delay in entering the workforce.

In 2012, some 40 percent of recent college graduates were working in jobs that did not require a college degree and 40 percent reported working in jobs that were not closely related to their degrees.[17] According to U.S. Department of Labor data, more than one million retail sales staff and 115,000 janitors and cleaners are college graduates.[18]

There is growing concern over the large debts many students and their families incur while pursuing, often unsuccessfully, college degrees. Total student debt exceeded $1 trillion in 2010, more than the nation's total credit card debt.[19] The median average student debt was $20,000 in 2011, about four times the average debt load of 20 years ago. "A sizeable number of the recession cohort, having graduated between 2009 and 2011, remain dependent on their families for some significant help in meeting daily financial obligations."[20]

Although it may be difficult for many parents and educators to admit, four-year college degrees are unnecessary for many occupations, for starting a business, and even for some high-paying jobs. Career and technical education in high school and college and apprenticeships may be better choices when they reflect a student's abilities, goals, and incentives. Two-year associate degrees and certificate programs are the fastest-growing areas of higher education not because they represent a lowering of expectations, but because they more closely correspond with the interests and genuine needs of many students.[21]

Students in a nine-month manufacturing training program near Chicago, for example, are quickly snapped up by employers, sometimes months before graduation, for starting salaries of $40,000 and likely jumps to $55,000 and $65,000 in less than two years.[22] Students who entered the program say they did so after comparing the cost of training against the cost of college as well as their likely starting salary after graduation.

Florida is adapting its curricula, tests, and graduation requirements to the needs of non-college-bound students without lowering standards or expectations. In 2013 the state adopted a plan giving students three ways to earn a high-school diploma: the "standard" diploma requiring 24 credit hours and passing end-of-course exams in language arts and Algebra I; a "scholar" diploma requiring at least one college-level course, a foreign language, and passing end-of-course tests in Algebra II, biology, and history; and a "merit" diploma requiring all the coursework for a standard diploma plus industry certification in one or more fields. Students seeking merit diplomas may take career education courses or enroll in work-related internships in place of advanced science and math classes.[23] The new plan marked a retreat from legislation passed in 2010 that added Algebra II, chemistry, and physics to basic graduation requirements. That law was subsequently seen as unfair to students not planning to go on to college and failing to prepare students with the skills and industry certifications they need to get jobs.

Florida Senate President Don Gaetz, who supported the new law, told reporters at the time it passed that the law did not make graduation requirements any less rigorous, but made them more appropriate to different types of students. "I'm a great believer in high standards. ... I also believe because students learn differently and have different aptitudes ... we have to devise curriculum that touches students where they are. ... We have to prepare students for real jobs in a real economy."[24]

Whether college-bound or not, high-school graduates are likely to be successful if they have strong communication skills. To succeed later in life in the workplace or college, adolescents must learn how to read and comprehend written instructions, solve problems, make decisions, resolve interpersonal conflicts, negotiate with others to achieve common goals, and actively listen. These skills are necessary to become a trustworthy colleague in the workplace, a reliable friend or spouse, and a good citizen. It is incumbent on K–12 schools, not the nation's colleges, to teach these skills before young adults graduate from high school.

Conclusion

Research has shown consistent and often substantial positive effects of properly designed reward systems on adolescent students' learning and high-school graduation rates. Teaching practices that have proven to motivate middle- and high-school students to learn include presenting lessons as opportunities for discovery and mastery rather than just following instructions, showing how new information and skills increase the student's "wealth," and making special efforts to show how a grade or disciplinary action is fair. These practices take student interests seriously and create rewards that are aligned with them.

Teaching students to "teach themselves" also has been shown to produce high achievement levels. Students can be shown how to plan their studying, monitor their progress, and seek out sources of information on their own. By making learning faster, self-teaching lowers the cost (in student time and effort) of learning, making it more attractive to students who are increasingly aware of the value of their time. New technologies make possible classes such as Brainology that blend online courses, videos, and classroom instruction to motivate students to solve problems or, in the case of Lego Mindstorms, to build something (robots) with their new knowledge and skills.

Finally, many high schools have been too insistent on academic college preparation for all students and have neglected career and technical education. This is understandable given the liberal arts background of most educators and the high hopes of many parents, but it is unfair to students who are not college-bound. An emphasis on practical knowledge and skills is likely to lower dropout rates and better prepare those students for certification training or job opportunities following graduation from high school. Florida's recent adoption of three paths to a high-school diploma is one way to achieve this without lowering academic standards.

Notes

1. Barry J. Zimmerman, "A Social Cognitive View of Self-Regulated Academic Learning," *Journal of Educational Psychology* 81, no. 3 (September 1989): 329–39.

2. Jacquelynne S. Eccles, Carol Midgley, Alan Wigfield, Christy M. Buchanan, David Reuman, Constance Flanagan, and Douglas Mac Iver, "Development During Adolescence: The Impact of Stage-Environment Fit on Young Adolescents' Experiences in Schools and in Families," *American Psychologist* 48, no. 2 (February 1993): 90–101.

3. Laurence Steinberg, "Autonomy, Conflict, and Harmony in the Family Relationship," in S.S. Feldman and G.R. Elliott, eds., *At the Threshold: The Developing Adolescent* (Cambridge, MA: Harvard University Press, 1993), pp. 255–76.

4. Julian L. Simon, *Effort, Opportunity, and Wealth* (New York, NY: Basil Blackwell Ltd., 1987).

5. The summary in the box incorporates our thoughts on why these features are effective and not necessarily the authors' thoughts or specific words.

6. Goal-setting, on the other hand, sometimes involves putting into students' heads things that weren't there before. We addressed that in Chapter 4.

7. Erin Macey, Janet Deckera, and Suzanne Eckesa, "The Knowledge Is Power Program (KIPP): An Analysis of One Model's Efforts to Promote Achievement in Underserved Communities," *Journal of School Choice* 3, no. 3 (2009).

8. Center on Educational Governance, University of Southern California, "KIPP Bayview Academy: Paycheck Program," http://www.uscrossier.org/ceg/products-and-services/promising-practices-compendium/education-programs-of-charter-schools/kipp-bayview-academy-paycheck-program/.

9. Interview with Mike Feinberg, co-founder of KIPP, "Making Schools Work with Hedrick Smith," PBS, undated, http://www.pbs.org/makingschoolswork/sbs/kipp/feinberg.html.

10. *Ibid.*

11. Theresa A. Thorkildsen, Algis Sodonis, and Lisa White-McNulty, "Epistemology and Adolescents' Conceptions of Procedural Justice in School," *Journal of Educational Psychology* 96, no. 2 (June 2004): 347–59.

12. See http://www.mindsetworks.com/, viewed on March 10, 2013.

13. See http://mindstorms.lego.com/en-us/Default.aspx, viewed on March 10, 2013.

14. http://www.khanacademy.org/.

15. James J. Heckman, John Eric Humphries, and Nicholas S. Mader, "The GED," *NBER Working Paper No. 16064*, June 2010, http://www.nber.org/papers/w16064.

16. It also is wrong to ignore the adverse effects on the nation's colleges and universities from the flood of academically unmotivated students unqualified for college studies. See

Richard K. Vedder, *Going Broke by Degree: Why College Costs Too Much* (Washington, DC: American Enterprise Institute for Public Policy Research, 2004).

17. Charley Stone, Carl Van Horn, and Cliff Zukin, "Chasing the American Dream: Recent College Graduates and the Great Recession," John J. Heldrich Center for Workforce Development, Rutgers University, May 2012, p. 7, http://www.heldrich.rutgers.edu/sites/default/files/content/Chasing_American_Dream_R eport.pdf.

18. Richard Vedder, "The Wages of Unemployment," *The Wall Street Journal*, January 15, 2013.

19. Charley Stone *et al.*, *supra* note 17, p. 10.

20. *Ibid.*, p. 21.

21. Caroline Porter, "Seeking a Shortcut to a Job," *The Wall Street Journal*, July 16, 2013, p. A3.

22. Parija Kavilanz, "Nine months in trade school. Job guaranteed," CNN Money, March 14, 2012, http://money.cnn.com/2012/03/14/ smallbusiness/trade-schools/index.htm.

23. Danny Valentine, "Blavatt Expresses Concerns Over Different Designations for High School Diplomas," *Tampa Bay Times*, April 27, 2013.

24. Katie Tammen, "New Law Changes High School Graduation Standards," NWFDailyNews.com, April 22, 2013.

PART THREE

Using Rewards to Accelerate Learning

8

Tests with Rewards

Our thesis up to this point has been that rewards work best when they are closely aligned with SMART goals (Specific, Measurable, Attainable, Realistic, and Time-bound). Testing for academic achievement is a critical part of the rewards process because it provides measurement, telling both the educator and the learner if goals are being achieved or what needs to be changed to make them achievable. Tests can be tailored to learners of every age and rewards can be attached to the test results.

The use of tests in K–12 education, while supported by parents and even students, is controversial in schools of education and therefore in teachers' lounges. In this chapter we review what critics of tests say, rebut the most common criticisms, and present best practices for attaching rewards to tests. We also describe the new (new for K–12 education, that is) technology of adaptive online testing and the importance of independent test audits.

Critics of Tests

Critics of rewards fiercely criticize standardized tests. For example, Alfie Kohn argued, "anyone who requires a formal test to know what is going on may need to reconsider the approach to instruction being used and whether he or she is talking too much and listening too little."[1] Monty Neil, executive director of FairTest, criticized the widespread use of tests, particularly the Massachusetts Comprehensive Assessment System, despite the state's repeated first place on the National Assessment of Educational Progress.[2] At a 1991 press conference organized by the American

Educational Research Association (AERA), a group composed mainly of education professors presented a long list of objections to the use of standardized tests, especially those connected to rewards for high scores.[3] Among their complaints: reliance on tests discourages teachers from teaching topics that don't appear on the tests; tests tap only "lower-order" thinking skills; and tests are unfair to minorities and women, costly in terms of money and time, and overused in the United States compared with other countries.

At best, the professors' criticisms apply only to poorly designed and administered tests. A frequent complaint about No Child Left Behind, a federal government education program, is that it relies too heavily on testing and has led to the adoption of "teacher-proof" curricula, or curricula so focused on specific learning outcomes that teachers were forbidden from making alterations in response to their own experience and understanding of their students' needs.[4] But the fact that tests sometimes are used poorly does not support wider criticism of their use as part of effective incentive programs.

Test critics ignore hundreds of published, well-designed studies complete with comparison groups that show the benefits of tests. Richard Phelps recently conducted a meta-analysis of the voluminous research and statistical analysis of the effects of standardized tests. His findings are summarized in the table on the following page.

Refuting the Critics
Six of the most frequent criticisms of standardized tests are presented below with rebuttals.[5]

Does testing take valuable time away from instruction?

Not when it is used correctly. Regular testing helps teachers determine if students have learned course material and are able to move on to more advanced skills and subject matter. Test results therefore *save* classroom time by helping teachers avoid needlessly reviewing or repeating lessons. Frequent testing increases the productivity of time spent on instruction by encouraging students to pay attention in class and do homework soon after it is assigned rather than "cramming" just before an exam. Well-designed tests encourage students to think through and practice material on their own time, either at school or at home.

Benefits of Standardized Tests

- Setting incentivized goals and measuring progress increases student motivation and performance in school achievement as well as sports and work settings.

- In school and college classes, frequent testing, including brief daily testing, results in greater learning.

- Giving students detailed analyses of their test results helps them identify their weaknesses and increases their learning; computer-assisted testing and information processing makes this quicker and more feasible.

- Learning is reinforced and enhanced by offering students overviews and details on what they have done well.

- Using tests to verify that students have mastered or nearly mastered specific content before introducing new material yields better results than traditional teaching that assumes a high degree of mastery.

- When studies focus on language learning, frequent testing has intensified and increased the speed with which students learn new languages.

Source: Richard Phelps "The Rich, Robust Research Literature on Testing's Achievement Benefits," in Richard P. Phelps, ed., *Defending Standardized Testing* (Mahwah, NJ: Lawrence Erlbaum Associates Publishers, 2005), pp. 55–90. See the source for original phrasing of these points.

Do testing programs divert scarce dollars from other more important uses such as classroom instruction?

No. The cost of testing is trivial compared to other school expenditures. Dollars spent on commercial firms for services including standardized testing, standards setting, and accountability reporting was less than 0.1 percent of total spending on K–12 education in 2000, amounting to only $5.81 per student on average.[6] It is doubtful that any other major enterprise in the U.S. spends a smaller percentage of its total budget measuring its outputs. New technology, moreover, is reducing the cost of testing as well as the amount of time teachers must spend calculating test scores and interpreting the results.[7]

Do standardized tests fail to cover important subject matter?

This criticism misrepresents the intent and value of most tests. A good multiple-choice test necessarily asks questions pertaining only to a small fraction of the content and skills a student is expected to acquire. It is not a checklist of all the things a student should know. Such tests can quickly and reliably sample much more content than a few essay questions. Just as a telephone poll of a small percentage of registered voters can produce reliable estimates of vote totals on election day, so can a multiple-choice test generate a good estimate of a student's overall achievement.

Do tests overemphasize factual knowledge and low-level skills?

Dismissing the importance of factual knowledge is part of the "progressive" education philosophy that lies beneath most objections to testing, but it is a view not shared by parents and employers. Multiple-choice tests, moreover, are used successfully for licensing advanced professions such as law and medicine, providing proof that such tests can measure highly advanced knowledge, understanding, and skills. Tests assessing complex achievement can require respondents to select the best idea from a group of different and compelling positions and identify the best reason for action, the best interpretation of a set of ideas, or the best application of important principles.[8]

Does testing place excessive pressure on students?

Some students find taking tests so stressful that it disrupts their study habits and ability to focus on the questions being asked. Too much focus on a single high-stakes test can be counterproductive even for students who don't react this way. But with these concerns in mind, policymakers can expand or contract testing requirements based on feedback from parents and educators. For example, Texas rolled back from 15 to five the number of tests required for K–12 students in 2013 following protests from educators and parents.[9] Teachers can relieve students' stress by explaining the purpose of the tests is to make learning in the future easier. Giving frequent short quizzes and low-consequence tests can accustom students to taking tests. Remediation efforts and second-chance exams can minimize the degree to which students feel they are unfairly punished for scoring poorly on a single exam. Experience in taking low- and high-stakes tests helps students prepare for college entry tests as well as job entry tests, professional examinations for entry into law and medical schools, and professional licensing tests.

Does testing threaten or undermine the confidence of teachers?

Teacher opposition to tests often is based on past experiences with poorly designed tests that were difficult to administer or time-consuming to score and interpret, or tests that were not aligned with the curriculum. No doubt, such tests still exist and fuel teacher opposition to proposals to rely more heavily on test results. But over time, as tests are improved and the curriculum is altered to enable students to anticipate questions and answer them correctly, teacher opposition should diminish. Good tests help teachers measure their student's performance, an indispensable part of planning lessons and improving instruction techniques.

Best Practices
In previous chapters, the impact of a specific reward on academic achievement often was measured by changes in the number of students taking an optional test or passing a test required for advancement or their scores. From this literature as well as the work of authors who specifically address the best design of reward systems, we find agreement on best practices that fall into five general categories.

Testing for Grade Promotion

Requiring students to pass tests before advancing them to the next grade level can be a powerful incentive for paying attention in class, reviewing and rehearsing what was learned, and making a focused effort to show progress toward academic goals. Teachers benefit because such tests help ensure that all the students in a classroom at the beginning of a school year have the necessary skills to begin the year at grade level. Such tests are rarely used for each grade promotion decision, though a number of states require students to pass tests to graduate from elementary to middle school and then from middle school to high school. Some states, such as California, require annual tests of all students but prohibit basing grade-to-grade promotion decisions solely on test results.

What if students fail the required tests? A program used by the Chicago Public Schools gave students the choice between being retained in a grade or taking a sharply focused six-week summer course and then taking a grade-level examination for promotion.[10] Independent researchers found that students who attended the six-week program made as much as a year-and-a-half of achievement progress. At a cost of six weeks of intensive work, the students saved themselves, teachers, and taxpayers a year of inefficient remediation.

Testing for Graduation

Requiring students to pass tests before awarding them a diploma can create positive incentives for improved behavior and performance in high school. Such tests send signals to students, teachers, parents, college admissions officers, and employers that a diploma certifies an accomplished standard of achievement. This belief in turn creates incentives for positive behavior by each group: students work harder to graduate knowing their diplomas are viewed as meaningful achievements by others; parents are given a goal they can encourage their children to reach; and college admissions officers and employers can reward students who earn their degrees by giving them preferential treatment in admissions and hiring decisions.

John Bishop's research on 17 states that require such tests showed they increase mathematics and science achievement and lead to good habits such as completing homework on time and talking with parents about schoolwork. Other researchers are less certain, expressing concern that such tests reduce the motivation of students already struggling with coursework to finish high school.[11] Creating alternative paths to a diploma, as Florida has done (see Chapter 7), is a possible solution to this potential problem.

Rather than requiring all students to complete their final four years of schooling, policymakers should allow advanced students to take high-school exit exams early. Passing comprehensive content-based exams would ensure these students mastered the high-school academic curriculum.[12] Given reasonably rigorous standards, exit exams could reduce the need for remedial instruction in colleges and prepare non-college-bound students for technical training, apprenticeships, or employment.

Test Incentives for Young Children

Young children can be encouraged to prepare for and take tests by receiving points, stickers, praise, and other small rewards for good scores. Tests teach children that goals and progress toward their achievement are measurable, that measurement can be objective, and that good performance often is rewarded. Rewards can be readily tailored to the interests and needs of children, something parents and observant teachers are usually able to do.

One stay-at-home mom capitalized on children's enthusiasm for token rewards by developing a point system to reward her children and their friends for passing short comprehension tests on books they read at their leisure. Her project grew to become the Accelerated Reader Program, which is available in about half of the schools in the U.S.[13]

Accelerated Reader consists of a search system that helps teachers select books suited to a student's interests and reading ability, five-item tests on more than 30,000 books generally available in school and community libraries, and a computer test with instant scoring. As students become stronger readers, they are encouraged to read more difficult books because points are awarded in proportion to the difficulty of the book and the number of correct answers. The program, which costs only $100 per year per student, keeps a detailed record of each student's progress, minimizing the amount of bookkeeping required by teachers and parents. While not intended to take the place of in-class instruction, Accelerated Reader has shown excellent results in a number of rigorous (control-group) studies conducted by independent scholars.[14]

Test Incentives for Adolescents

As children move into adolescence, rewards must become larger to account for the growing "wealth" of the students, the rising value of their time, and their ability to defer gratification and be motivated by rewards that are further in the future. Token awards and public recognition attached to tests can still incentivize academic progress, but financial rewards and increased responsibility such as permission to use a car or to choose other activities may be more motivating.

In Chapter 3 we reviewed research by John Bishop, Victor Lavy, and Roland Fryer Jr. on how adolescents respond positively to being paid to take or score high on Michigan's Educational Achievement Program (MEAP) tests, Advanced Placement exams, and the New York Regents Examination. In Chapter 7 we reported how KIPP Academies pay middle-school students with "KIPP dollars" for effort, good behavior, and completed homework. We also saw how strategies for "self-teaching" reward students by lowering the students' cost of learning and allowing them to compete with other students in learning programs such as Lego Mindstorms.

Many teenagers are able to see a connection between the tests they must take and possible careers, such as positions in medicine, science, or law enforcement. Some charter schools have shown remarkable success by getting adolescents to focus on the importance of attending college after graduation and the need to meet college admission standards. Students who are not college-bound can be incentivized to stay in school and graduate by giving them a path to a high-school diploma that gives them the experience or industry certifications they need to get the jobs they want after graduating. Florida's three paths – standard, scholar, and merit – show how this can be done without lowering graduation requirements.

Tests and Advanced Accomplishment

Grade-level advancement and high-school graduation exams typically establish low thresholds that students must pass rather than high targets to which they should aspire. Advanced academic accomplishment such as honors courses, showing high foreign language proficiency, and passing Advanced Placement (AP) exams requires much more from students. Programs that encourage students to make extra effort include making access to such courses convenient and free, teaching them in especially comfortable or high-status classrooms, and supplying tutoring and other support activities. Schools can support student clubs based on the coursework and interests of high-achieving students, such as debate and foreign languages. Tournaments, class trips, parties, and other activities organized for high achievers can take the place of some of the school activities dominated by lower-achieving students.

Most students and parents are aware of AP programs and the possibility of attaining college credits, but they do not fully comprehend how large the financial rewards can be when a student places out of one or more college courses. With ever-rising college tuition levels, the savings can reach $40,000 or more. Teachers and school administrators can make this incentive much more powerful by documenting the dollar value of college credits and describing how much past students and their parents saved by taking the exams.

Students and teachers also can be motivated by modest financial awards each time a student passes an AP exam, as the O'Donnell Foundation's program in Dallas demonstrated. Recall from our discussion of the program in Chapter 3 that paying students and teachers $100 for each passing score and providing a $2,500 stipend to teachers who undergo training to teach the courses increased the number of students who passed AP exams more than 12-fold.[15] Large-scale expansion of the O'Donnell example would seem likely to reduce the time students require to gain diplomas as well as college degrees, and in the process significantly cut the costs of their education.

Adaptive Online Testing

As mentioned earlier, new technology is reducing the cost of testing and saving teachers time by automating test administration, scoring, and interpreting the results. This is part of a bigger transformation technology is bringing to K–12 education that we describe in greater depth in Chapter 10. The following observations focus on how online adaptive testing is giving testing with rewards greater importance than ever before.

Adaptive online tests are typically administered via the Internet from a central site outside the classroom and school. Students take the tests alone or in a group depending on the number of Internet-connected computers available to the class. Large numbers of test questions are stored in databases and a computer program uses a student's performance on each item to select the next item. Each correct answer leads to a more difficult question while wrong answers lead to easier questions. This process quickly reveals the student's ability level, reducing the number of questions a student has to answer and cutting testing time by as much as two-thirds.

Adaptive testing has been used for some years for college, graduate, and professional school admission, providing valuable experience for the companies that now offer the service to K–12 schools. Where paper-and-pencil tests may take weeks to be scored and returned, adaptive tests provide instant scores and quick, detailed reports for teachers to pinpoint gaps in students' understanding. Schools can receive reports comparing each student's performance with class, school, district, and state results. Because adaptive tests take less time, they may be given more frequently. Students cannot cheat as easily on adaptive tests as they can on traditional paper-and-pencil tests since nearby students are usually answering different questions.[16]

The Khan Academy, a free library of online videos and problem sets, uses an adaptive learning system for its widely praised tutorials on mathematics and other subjects.[17] Students watch short videos on core mathematics concepts, starting at the beginning with addition, subtraction, and the idea of numbers. They then take tests to determine how well they have understood the material. The software tracks the errors the student makes and cues up the next set of videos and concepts to target the student's weaknesses or to move on to more advanced lessons. As students progress, they earn badges and points for concepts they have mastered.

Independent Test Audits

A critical problem facing those who would align rewards with test results is the temptation faced by policymakers and educators to make the tests easier to create the appearance of progress or to hide declining performance. The reliance of No Child Left Behind on state-designed tests made this problem especially apparent as states lowered their standards and schools manipulated the administration of tests in order to meet the law's achievement requirements.

Many states make their tests easier over time to produce the appearance of student progress. Others allow the tests to remain unchanged and their content items become better known in schools, thus enabling "teaching to the test" and making it appear that student achievement is rising. Still other states introduce a new curriculum and set of tests every three or four years, conveniently making it impossible to compare academic progress over periods of time that would show the actual trends in student achievement. And if all this weren't bad enough, some educators actually conspire and cheat to avoid reporting a lack of progress.[18]

To minimize such problems, accounting and auditing procedures analogous to those in business could be established for schools, districts, and whole states (or at least problematic ones). Independent auditing firms could review and report on plans and the execution of testing programs. When fraud is detected, perpetrators could face the same types of consequences as those in business – that is, firing and prosecution for fraud. In schools suspected of fraud, the independent auditors would administer the tests as well.

Conclusion

Critics of tests present a litany of objections, many of them based on past experiences with poorly designed tests, but ways to improve tests are well specified. Some students respond poorly to high-stakes exams, but there are ways to mitigate their anxiety. Simply letting them avoid tests during their K–12 careers isn't doing them any favors since tests with consequences will be a challenge they will face later in higher education and adult life. Some states and schools have manipulated their tests in order to avoid federal sanctions or to escape accountability to voters, but this is only an argument for relying on national tests or turning to independent agencies to administer and audit testing.

Tests are essential if rewards are to be used to accelerate learning since tests measure progress toward academic goals. The extensive research reviewed by Richard Phelps shows how setting goals and measuring progress increases student motivation and performance, frequent testing results in greater learning, and giving students detailed analyses of their test results helps them identify their weaknesses and increases their learning. Many cities and states are using tests with rewards successfully in five general areas: for grade advancement, for graduation, with young children, with adolescents, and for advanced academic achievement. Adaptive online testing and independent test audits promise to cut the time and cost of testing and to boost dramatically the power of rewards to accelerate learning.

Notes

1. Alfie Kohn, *Punished by Rewards: The Trouble with Gold Stars, Incentive Plans, A's, Praise, and Other Bribes* (Boston, MA: Houghton Mifflin, Co., 1993), p. 203.

2. Monty Neil, testimony, June 23, 2009, http://blip.tv/film-our-way-films/monty-neil-mcas-hearing June-23-2009-2547640.

3. Richard P. Phelps, "Why Testing Experts Hate Testing," in Williamson M. Evers and Herbert J. Walberg, eds., *Testing Student Learning, Evaluating Teaching Effectiveness* (Stanford, CA: Hoover Institution Press, 2004), p. 29.

4. Thomas Ahn and Jacob L. Vigdor, "Were All Those Standardized Tests for Nothing? The Lessons of No Child Left Behind," American Enterprise Institute, May 2013.

5. This section is adapted from Herbert Walberg, *Tests, Testing, and Genuine School Reform* (Stanford, CA: Hoover Institution Press, 2011), Chapter 2.

6. Caroline M. Hoxby, "The Cost of Accountability," in Williamson M. Evers and Herbert J. Walberg, eds., *School Accountability* (Stanford, CA: Hoover Institution Press, 2002), pp. 47–74.

7. See Herbert Walberg, *supra* note 5, Chapter 9.

8. Norman E. Gronlund and C. Keith Waugh, *Assessment of Student Achievement, 9th edition* (Boston, MA: Allyn and Bacon, 2008).

9. Erik Robelen, "Testing Rolled Back, Graduation Path Revised Under Texas Bill," *Education Week*, May 28, 2013.

10. Melissa Roderick, Jenny Nagaoka, and Elaine M. Allensworth, "Is the Glass Half-full or Mostly Empty? Ending Social Promotion in Chicago," in Edward H. Haertel and Joan Herman, eds., *Uses and Misuses of Data for Educational Accountability and Improvement; The 104th Yearbook for the National Society for the Study of Education, Part 2* (Malden, MA: National Society for the Study of Education, 2005), pp. 223–59.

11. Center on Education Policy, "State High School Exit Exams: A Policy in Transition," Graduate School of Education and Human Development, The George Washington University, September 2012.

12. See the discussion of curriculum-based external exams in Chapter 3.

13. Details on the company and the program can be found at http://www.renlearn.com/ar/.

14. Keith J. Topping and Terry D. Paul, "Computer-Assisted Assessment of Practice at Reading: A Large-Scale Survey Using Accelerated Reader Data," *Reading and Writing Quarterly* 15 (1999): 213–31; Stacy R. Vollans, Keith J. Topping, and Ryka M. Evans, "Computerized Self-Assessment of Reading Comprehension with the Accelerated Reader: Action Research," *Reading and Writing Quarterly* 15 (1999): 197–211; John A. Nunnery, Steven M. Ross, and Aaron McDonald, "A Randomized Experimental Evaluation of the Impact of Accelerated Reader/Reading Renaissance Implementation on

Reading Achievement in Grades 3 to 6," *Journal of Education for Students Placed at Risk* 11, no. 1 (2006): 1–18.

15. C. Kirabo Jackson, "Cash for Test Scores: The Impact of the Texas Advanced Placement Incentive Program," *Education Next* 8, no. 4 (Fall 2008). See also Herbert J. Walberg, "Incentivized School Standards Work," *Education Week*, November 4, 1998, p. 48.

16. Cheating is still possible, though. See Cameron McWhirter, "High-Tech Cheaters Pose Test," *The Wall Street Journal*, June 11, 2013, p. A3.

17. See www.khanacademy.org.

18. For example, see Ned Resnikov, "Atlanta Cheating Scandal Puts National Education Policy on Trial," MSNBC, http://tv.msnbc.com/2013/04/01/atlanta-cheating-scandal-puts-national-education-policy-on-trial/, viewed on June 10, 2013.

9

Rewarding Good Teachers

More than two centuries ago, Adam Smith wrote that "the rivalship of competitors" and emulation of those who have succeeded are two potent reasons why people "execute [their] work with a certain degree of exactness."[1] We've seen how students respond positively when allowed to compete for rewards. How about teachers?

Proposals to pay teachers based on the performance of their students face stiff resistance for several reasons. Since many of us find learning to be a pleasurable activity, we assume teaching is as well and jump to the conclusion that internal motivation dominates the choices made by teachers. There is no doubt that most teachers are attracted to their careers by a sense of calling and not as a route to personal wealth.[2] Offering some teachers financial rewards but withholding them from others may seem crass or offensive since it implies some aren't already trying as hard as they can to help their students learn. The difficulty of discerning how much learning is attributable to the efforts of individual teachers and not their colleagues, their students' innate abilities, or parents and other influences outside the school raises questions about how performance-based pay could be calculated and whether it would incentivize the desired behavior.

We can start our inquiry into performance-based pay by reviewing evidence regarding the variability in teacher effectiveness and the impact it has on student achievement. This literature suggests large increases in student learning could occur if the behavior of teachers could be changed. We then examine the problem of teacher burnout – teachers who feel disrespected, trapped in their careers, and denied access to the tools or policies they need to perform at higher levels. For these teachers, the current system of teacher compensation plainly isn't working. After reviewing how performance-based pay works in other occupations, we present a series of best practices based on experiences of schools in the U.S. and elsewhere.

Impact of Good Teachers

Not all teachers are equally effective in their classrooms. Researchers have found teacher quality varies considerably from teacher to teacher and among schools, and this variation in turn has a significant measurable impact on student achievement. Among the earliest researchers to find this was Eric Hanushek, now a senior fellow at the Hoover Institution of Stanford University.[3] Based on data on approximately 1,800 students in Gary, Indiana, he estimated the city's most effective teachers boosted their students' learning by about 1.5 grade-level equivalents a year while the least effective teachers produced only 0.5 grade-level equivalents of growth. His research originally was published in 1971, and he has frequently revisited the issue using different databases and methodologies.[4]

Other researchers have found similar effects. William Sanders and June Rivers, for example, found students who had encountered teachers at or above the 80th percentile of performance for three consecutive years performed 50 percentile points higher on student achievement tests than students who encountered teachers in the bottom 20th percentile for three years.[5] Douglas O. Staiger and Jonah E. Rockoff, using data from public schools in Los Angeles and New York City, found "the standard deviation across teachers in their impact on student achievement gains is on the order of 0.1 to 0.2 student-level standard deviations, which would improve the median student's test score 4 to 8 percentiles in a single year."[6]

Writing in 2010, Staiger and Rockoff acknowledged that research on teacher effects rests on statistical assumptions that are "extraordinarily strong and rarely tested," but they contend there is strong research support for the conclusion "that the magnitude of variation in teacher effects is driven by real differences in teacher quality."[7] They find estimates by different researchers tend to be consistent in a variety of circumstances. Teacher effects on achievement are also consistent with evaluations made by school principals and other professional educators, and studies based on random assignments of teachers to classrooms show teacher effects similar to those of non-experimental studies.

These findings have prompted a large number of studies seeking to determine what distinguishes a "highly effective" from a "least effective" teacher. Surprisingly, researchers have found teacher characteristics such as post-graduate degrees, years of experience (beyond the first year or two), and licensing examination scores "do not represent teacher quality" and do not predict how a teacher's students will perform.[8] This finding poses problems for those who would seek to hire only "high-quality" teachers or dismiss "low-quality" teachers since teachers in both categories may have identical training and apparent qualifications.

Rather than being a source of despair for reformers seeking to accelerate student learning, these findings should be a cause for optimism. In Chapter 1 we reported research showing that self-discipline, perseverance, and "grit" play a bigger role than innate intelligence in predicting academic success. This means innate intelligence does not limit who might benefit from incentives or impose a ceiling on how much such incentives can enhance academic performance. Similarly, we find teachers can be highly effective regardless of their training, lack of experience, or performance on licensing exams. Some teachers already are highly effective. But nearly all teachers can become highly effective. They need to be appropriately taught and incentivized.

Teacher Burnout

If education, training, experience, and other standard measures of teacher quality don't correlate with success in the classroom, why aren't more teachers highly effective? One major reason is because millions of teachers are unhappy in their current positions.[9] Frederick M. Hess, a former teacher and currently director of education studies at the American Enterprise Institute, recently painted a grim picture of what it is like to be a public school teacher in America:

> Teachers are hired, essentially for life, through drawn-out recruiting processes that pay little attention to merit and alienate many highly qualified candidates. Little or nothing about teachers' or administrators' performance affects their career prospects or job security. Educators who propose new approaches or new efficiencies are treated with suspicion by district officials and must run a gauntlet of official and cultural resistance in order to try anything new. There is little systemic recognition for excellent educators, while pay, perks, and assignments are distributed

primarily on the basis of longevity. The result is a culture of public schooling in which educators learn to keep their heads down, play defense, and avoid causing waves.[10]

Other researchers report that hiring and retaining good teachers is handicapped by "disparities in pay and working conditions, interstate barriers to teachers' mobility, inadequate recruitment incentives, bureaucratic hiring systems that discourage qualified applicants, transfer policies that can slow hiring and allocate staff inequitably, and financial incentives to hire cheaper, less qualified teachers."[11] Little wonder, then, that more than 30 percent of new teachers leave the profession within five years. This churning "results in a constant influx of inexperienced teachers" resulting in "insufficient preparation and support of new teachers, poor working conditions, and uncompetitive salaries."[12]

These conditions have led to an epidemic of "teacher burnout," which Anthony Dworkin, a sociologist at the University of Houston, defines as "a response to job stress and related to a sense of meaninglessness and powerlessness" and "a malady of human service professionals who are denied professional autonomy, status, and respect."[13] Dworkin has conducted surveys showing teacher burnout has risen following each of three school reform "waves' since 1983: legislated standardization and competency testing, decentralization and site-based decision-making, and high-stakes testing with accountability.[14] Dworkin found teachers in 2012 reported feeling stressed at twice the rate as those in 2002.[15]

Anecdotal evidence of teacher burnout abounds. A long-time Milwaukee teacher wrote in 1994, "Very common are teachers who at one time were good, but after years of bureaucratic nonsense and dwindling morale, do not much like their job anymore."[16] A 1997 *San Antonio Express-News* Sunday Insight section, titled "Schoolhouse Blues," described the same feelings among teachers and administrators in Texas.[17] The authors noted the constant changing of programs creates panic, low morale, and burnout. A letter-writer to *Education Week* in 1998 similarly reported "teachers are in a virtual state of panic, caught between crushing district mandates and the need to raise standardized test scores."[18]

These anecdotes all date prior to 2001, the year the No Child Left Behind Act was passed. Lisa Singleton-Rickman reported in 2009, "with stricter-than-ever accountability laws through the federal No Child Left Behind and significantly more paperwork, teachers suffer burnout more quickly than they did 10 years ago."[19]

Is teacher burnout an unavoidable part of the teaching profession? To answer this question, Greg Forster and Christian D'Andrea analyzed data from the 2007–2008 Schools and Staffing Survey (SASS), a national survey of teachers and principals conducted by the U.S. Department of Education.[20] They found compelling evidence that teacher burnout is mostly a public school phenomenon. Forster and D'Andrea wrote:

> Private school teachers consistently report having better working conditions than public school teachers across a wide variety of measurements. Most prominently, private schools provide teachers with more classroom autonomy, a more supportive school climate, and better student discipline. It appears that the dysfunctions of the government school system – long evident in mediocre educational outcomes – are a problem for teachers as well as for students.

These professional opinions, survey data, and anecdotes reveal that many public-school teachers under-perform in the classroom. They feel mistreated by the current system of recruiting, paying, and managing teachers.

Performance-based Pay

Performance-based pay is pervasive outside the world of public K–12 education. An estimated 75 percent of the U.S. workforce is paid at least partly based on performance.[21] The late Nobel economist Robert William Fogel wrote, "even in occupations such as surgery, which attracts some of the most diligent and talented persons in the nation, there are significant variations in hours worked and in skill. As a result, those in the top tenth of the distribution of surgeons' incomes earn six times as much as those in the bottom tenth."[22]

Performance-based pay is common in higher education. Labor economist Michael Podgursky writes, "there are large differences in pay between faculty by teaching fields. Faculty pay structures in most higher education institutions are flexible. Starting pay is usually market driven, and institutions will often match counteroffers for more-senior faculty whom they wish to retain. Merit or performance-based pay is commonplace."[23] Also common in higher education is the use of prizes to reward high achievement and incentivize others to compete for future awards. Some of the more notable prizes include the Abel Prize (in mathematics, $1 million), Lasker Award (in medical sciences, $250,000), MacArthur Foundation Fellowship awards for "creative work" ($500,000), Nobel Prizes ($1.2 million, launched in 1901), Shaw Prizes (in astronomy, life science and medicine, and mathematical sciences, $1 million), and Wolf Prizes (in various sciences, $100,000). In recent years several new prizes with large financial rewards have been launched: the Fundamental Physics Prize and Breakthrough Prize in Life Sciences (each $3 million), Tang Prize (in sustainable development, biopharmaceutical science, Sinology, and rule of law, $1.7 million), Queen Elizabeth Prize for Engineering ($1.5 million), and Blavatnik Award (for young scientists, $250,000).[24]

The wide ranges in compensation seen in many professions and the use of cash awards to recognize and promote high achievement differ dramatically from the way teachers are paid in public K–12 schools. Nearly all public school teachers are paid according to a "single-salary schedule" or "position-automatic system" that requires teachers with a given number of years of experience and education level to receive identical pay.[25] Except during the first few years of teaching, neither of these pay determinants is linked to student achievement. Even special pay for difficult-to-recruit-for subjects such as science and mathematics and "combat pay" for teaching in difficult schools are rare. As a result, underperforming teachers get paid the same as the best teachers and rarely lose their jobs. Ambitious, hardworking, fairness-conscious superior teachers resent that they earn no more than the least competent and laziest member of the faculty, which may cause them to scale back their own efforts or leave the profession entirely.[26]

Dale Ballou and Michael Podgursky say there is "no other profession where compensation and contract renewal are so largely divorced from evaluations of performance as they are in public school teaching."[27] In the current system, even the rare teacher salary incentives are a mixed blessing. They can motivate innovation and spur creativity, but they also can create tension among teachers.[28] Increased productivity doesn't raise a public school's merit pay funding or total budget. More money for one teacher can mean less for others. Since someone else's good evaluation can be bad for them, teachers become more reluctant to share ideas and materials, praise their colleagues, or work in teams.

Basing pay on performance does not mean other kinds of rewards should not be used. A survey of business managers conducted by a prominent business consulting group found respondents ranked three noncash motivators – "praise from immediate managers, leadership attention (for example, one-on-one conversations), and a chance to lead projects or task forces" – just as high as or higher than the three highest-rated financial incentives in the survey: cash bonuses, increased base pay, and stock or stock options.[29] Financial and nonfinancial incentives ought to be in the toolbox of every effective manager including school principals and other school leaders.

Even if most current teachers were internally motivated to enter the teaching profession, changing the way they are compensated may not affect their decisions to remain in the profession or attract more talented persons to become teachers. Indeed, changing teacher compensation may be necessary to attract the best and brightest to the profession. Dworkin, who is no fan of competition or rewards in K–12 education, found "teacher burnout has a minimal effect on student achievement and attendance"[30] in part because higher-performing teachers tend to have transferrable skills and are more likely to quit the teaching profession.[31] In other words, burned-out teachers don't affect student achievement and attendance because most of the good teachers who could raise student achievement have left the profession.

Raising teacher salaries, Dworkin admits, would have the effect of retaining some lower-quality and burned-out teachers.[32] His conclusion is striking, even though he fails to recognize that he is, in effect, endorsing performance-based pay for teachers: "It is likely that only when so many of the best and the brightest elect never to consider a career in public school teaching or quit after a short tenure in teaching, that one would expect to find, as we have, that teacher commitment has such a tiny effect upon student learning."[33]

North Carolina recently adopted legislation eliminating teacher tenure and automatic pay increases for master's degrees, making it a leader in the movement to remove the disincentives to teacher excellence.[34] But there is still a long way even for North Carolina to go before the promise of performance-based pay for teachers is realized. Many educators and some policy analysts say performance-based pay for student learning hasn't been sufficiently demonstrated to justify further study or use in schools. Yet, the achievement failures and rising costs of public schools suggest the opposite. Since performance-based pay is nearly universal in other occupations and professions, the burden of proof rests with those who defend the single-salary schedule. While spurious claims are made that performance-based pay is unfair to educators, the single-salary schedule is actually unfair to the millions of children in public schools who are subject to poor teaching and repeatedly failing schools.

Best Practices

Performance-based compensation is widely used outside the K–12 education sector, including by government. A robust literature on best practices can be applied, with some modifications, to teacher compensation.[35] An excellent guide to best practices is a 2006 report from the U.S. Merit Systems Protection Board, an independent, quasi-judicial agency in the executive branch. It recommends that performance-based compensation programs be designed around 12 "decision points" and that agencies contemplating such programs meet seven "requirements." Both lists appear in the table on the following page.

Performance-based pay for teachers has been debated, proposed, and attempted "in virtually every decade since the 1950s."[36] Unfortunately, little progress has been made in implementing the idea on a large scale. Teachers union opposition accounts for much of this failure[37] but also to blame was the absence, until recently, of longitudinal student test results and teacher panel data that could reliably connect an individual teacher's efforts to the academic progress of his or her students, a procedure called value-added modeling.[38] During the past decade, value-added modeling has informed small-scale experiments and pilot programs in several states including Arkansas, Illinois, New York, North Carolina, Tennessee, and Texas, and internationally in India, Israel, Kenya, and Mexico. Evaluations of these programs typically find modest positive effects on student achievement.[39]

Some possible best practices for performance-based pay for teachers derived from studies of these experiments and pilot programs[40] include:

■ Since conventional measures of teacher qualification fail to predict teacher effectiveness, principals and administrators should reward actual classroom performance rather than credentials.

■ Starting teachers whose performance results are below average should be let go quickly, after their first year or two of data are available for review, even at the risk of losing some teachers who might improve.[41]

Effective Pay-for-Performance Systems

Decision Points

1. Is the agency ready for pay for performance?

2. What are the goals of pay for performance?

3. Who should be paid for performance?

4. What should be the timing for implementing pay for performance?

5. What should be rewarded?

6. How should employees be rewarded?

7. How much pay should be contingent upon performance?

8. How should performance-based pay be funded?

9. How can costs be managed?

10. Who makes performance rating and pay decisions?

11. Who provides input to performance ratings?

12. How can agencies facilitate pay system integrity?

Agency Requirements

1. A culture that supports pay for performance

2. Effective and fair supervisors

3. A rigorous performance evaluation system

4. Adequate funding

5. A system of checks and balances to ensure fairness

6. Appropriate training for supervisors and employees

7. Ongoing system evaluation

Source: U.S. Merit Systems Protection Board, *Designing an Effective Pay for Performance Compensation System, A Report to the President and the Congress of the United States*, January 2006, http://www.mspb.gov/netsearch/viewdocs.aspx?docnumber=224104&version=224323&application=ACROBAT.

- Teacher effectiveness should be measured by value added – the change in the academic achievement of a teacher's class as measured by standardized tests – rather than absolute test levels or pass rates that could reflect student aptitude or the effects of teachers in prior school years.

- The average achievement gains of all students may be taken as the performance criterion rather than simply the percentage that crosses a particular minimum score or pass rate (called the "cut score"). This avoids encouraging educators to concentrate on students below the cut scores while neglecting other students.

- All teachers should be eligible for the reward offered, but only a subset of teachers should be rewarded in practice.

- The best incentive programs align teachers' raises and bonuses with student learning, but additional criteria may be used such as giving the principal's assessment half the weight of the overall performance rank.

- Principals also should be rewarded based on school performance to encourage them to take greater care in assessing teachers.

- Given the poor performance and high costs of public schools, large incentives seem to be in order. Making the incentive half the total compensation for both teachers and principals may be too much, but 5 percent seems too little.

- Reward systems "must align performance with ultimate outcomes and must be monitored closely to discourage gaming if not outright fraud in measured output."[42]

- Individual rewards must be balanced with school incentives, fostering a cooperative culture but not at the expense of free riding or some teachers unjustifiably riding on the coattails of others.

Conclusion

Research clearly demonstrates that teacher effectiveness varies considerably and that differences in teacher quality have major effects on student achievement. Since teacher effectiveness is not determined by post-graduate degrees, years of experience (beyond the first year or two), or scores on licensing exams, it follows that the behavior of teachers can be changed by incentives: nearly every teacher, regardless of training or experience, could be effective.

Many teachers are under-performing because the current system of hiring, paying, and managing teachers creates perverse incentives. Good teachers are not rewarded for their successes or additional efforts and ineffective teachers are rewarded with pay increases and pension benefits based solely on tenure, encouraging them to stay long after they have "burned out." Beginning teachers are granted tenure within a few years without consideration of their effectiveness, and once granted tenure they are difficult to terminate.

Performance-based pay is common in the private sector and in higher education. Experiments with performance-based pay for teachers have been moderately successful to date but typically have been seen only on small scales and often not informed by newly available data from value-added modeling. This creates an opportunity to implement performance-based pay on a much wider scale based on more reliable data than previously were available. Current research suggests this would lead to a considerable boost in student achievement.

Notes

1. Adam Smith, *The Wealth of Nations* (Indianapolis, IN: Liberty Press, 1976 [1776]), p. 760.

2. Anthony Gary Dworkin, *Teacher Burnout in the Public Schools: Structural Causes and Consequences for Children* (New York, NY: SUNY Press, 1987), p. 170.

3. Eric A. Hanushek, "Teacher Characteristics and Gains in Student Achievement: Estimation Using Micro Data," *American Economic Review* 61, no. 2 (1971): 280–88.

4. See Eric A. Hanushek, "The Economics of Schooling: Production and Efficiency in Public Schools," *Journal of Economic Literature* 24, no. 3 (1986): 1141–77; and by the same author, "The Trade-off between Child Quantity and Quality," *Journal of Political Economy* 100, no. 1 (1992): 84–117; "Assessing the Effects of School Resources on Student Performance: An Update," *Educational Evaluation and Policy Analysis* 19, no. 2 (1997): 141–64.

5. William L. Sanders and June C. Rivers, "Cumulative and Residual Effects of Teachers on Future Student Academic Achievement," Value-Added Research and Assessment Center, University of Tennessee, 1996.

6. Douglas O. Staiger and Jonah E. Rockoff, "Searching for Effective Teachers with Imperfect Information," *Journal of Economic Perspectives* 24, no. 3 (Summer 2010): 97. See also Jonah E. Rockoff, "The Impact of Individual Teachers on Student Achievement: Evidence from Panel Data," *American Economic Review* 94, no. 2 (2004): 247–52.

7. Douglas O. Staiger and Jonah E. Rockoff, *ibid.*, p. 100.

8. Eric A. Hanushek and Steven G. Rivkin, "Generalizations about Using Value-Added Measures of Teacher Quality," *American Economic Review* 100, no. 2, (May 2010): 267–71.

9. This section is adapted, with many changes, from Joseph L. Bast, Herbert J. Walberg, and Bruno Behrend, "How Teachers in Texas Would Benefit from Expanding School Choice," *Policy Brief*, The Heartland Institute, April 2011.

10. Frederick M. Hess, *Common Sense School Reform* (New York, NY: Palgrave Macmillan, 2004), p. 5.

11. Linda Darling-Hammond and Gary Sykes, "A Teacher Supply Policy for Education: How to Meet the 'Highly Qualified Teacher' Challenge," Chapter 7 in Noel Epstein, ed., *Who's in Charge Here? The Tangled Web of School Governance and Policy* (Washington, DC: Brookings Institution Press/Education Commission of the States, 2004), pp. 165–6.

12. *Ibid.*

13. A. Gary Dworkin, "Perspectives on Teacher Burnout and School Reform," *International Education Journal* 2, no. 2 (2001): 76, http://ehlt.flinders.edu.au/education/iej/articles/v2n2/dworkin/paper.pdf.

14. *Ibid.*, p. 69.

15. *Ibid.*

16. Michael Fischer, "A Betrayal of Teachers by Their Union," *Wisconsin Interest*, Fall/Winter 1994, p. 35.

17. Bill MacWhithey, "Good Teachers Tired of Battling the System," *San Antonio Express-News*, June 1, 1997, p. 1J.

18. Denis Udall, letter to the editor, *Education Week*, July 8, 1998, pp. 41, 43.

19. Lisa Singleton-Rickman, "Teacher Dropout Rate Higher than Students," TimesDaily.com, February 22, 2009.

20. Greg Forster and Christian D'Andrea, *Free to Teach: What America's Teachers Say About Teaching in Public and Private Schools* (Indianapolis, IN: The Friedman Foundation for Educational Choice, 2009). The latest SASS data are available at U.S. Department of Education, National Center for Education Statistics, "Schools and Staffing Survey (SASS)," http://nces.ed.gov/surveys/sass/, visited September 9, 2014.

21. Terry M. Moe, *Special Interest: Teachers Unions and America's Public Schools* (Washington, DC: Brookings Institution, 2011), p. 310.

22. Robert William Fogel, *The Fourth Great Awakening and the Future of Egalitarianism* (Chicago, IL: University of Chicago Press, 2002), p. 165.

23. Michael Podgursky, "A Market-Based Perspective on Teacher Compensation Reform," Chapter 4 in Matthew G. Springer, *Performance Incentives: Their Growing Impact on American K–12 Education* (Washington, DC: Brookings Institution, 2009), p. 70.

24. Zeeya Merali, "The New Nobels," *Nature* 498 (June 13, 2013): 152–4.

25. Terry M. Moe, *supra* note 21, pp. 179–80.

26. Caroline M. Hoxby and Andrew Leigh, "Pulled Away or Pushed Out? Explaining the Decline of Teacher Aptitude in the United States," *American Economic Review* 93 (2004): 236–40.

27. Dale Ballou and Michael Podgursky, *Teacher Pay and Teacher Quality* (Kalamazoo, MI: Upjohn Institute for Employment Research, 1997), p. 81.

28. Anthony Gary Dworkin and Merrill Townsend, "Teacher Burnout in the Face of Reform: Some Caveats in Breaking the Mold," Chapter 6 in Bruce A. Jones and Kathryn M. Borman, eds., *Investing in U.S. Schools: Directions for Educational Policy* (New York, NY: Ablex Publishing Company, 1994).

29. Martin Dewhurst, Matthew Guthridge, and Elizabeth Mohr, "Motivating People: Getting Beyond Money," McKinsey & Company, *McKinsey Quarterly*, November 2009.

30. Anthony Gary Dworkin, *supra* note 2, p. 150.

31. *Ibid.*, p. 126.

32. *Ibid.*, p. 171.

33. *Ibid.*

34. Stephanie Banchero and Meredith Rutland, "State Ends Teachers' Pay Boosts for Getting a Master's," *The Wall Street Journal*, July 27–28, 2018, p. A2.

35. Edward P. Lazear and Kathryn L. Shaw, *Personnel Economics* (Cambridge, MA: National Bureau of Economic Research, 2007).

36. Matthew G. Springer, "Rethinking Teacher Compensation Policies: Why Now, Why Again?" Chapter 1 in Matthew G. Springer, *supra* note 23, p. 4.

37. Terry M. Moe, *supra* note 21.

38. Daniel F. McCaffrey, Bing Han, and J.R. Lockwood, "Turning Student Test Scores into Teacher Compensation Systems," Chapter 6 in Matthew G. Springer, *supra* note 23, pp. 113–47.

39. Matthew G. Springer, *supra* note 23, Table 1-2, pp. 12–13, 17.

40. *Ibid.* See also Michael Kremer, Edward Miguel, and Rebecca Thornton, "Incentives to Learn," *Review of Economics and Statistics* 91 (2009): 437–56; Edward P. Lazear and Kathryn L. Shaw, "Personnel Economics: The Economist's View of Human Resources," *NBER Working Paper No. 13653,* November 2007, http://www.nber.org/papers/w13653; Michael J. Podgursky and Matthew G. Springer, "Teacher Performance Pay: A Review," *Working Paper No. 2006-01,* National Center on Performance Incentives, November 2006, https://my.vanderbilt.edu/performanceincentives/files/2012/10/.200601-PodgurskySpringer-PerformPay11.pdf.

41. Douglas O. Staiger and Jonah E. Rockoff, *supra* note 6, pp. 106ff.

42. Victor Lavy, "Using Performance-based Pay to Improve the Quality of Teachers," *The Future of Children* 17, no. 1 (Spring 2007): 87.

10

Rewards and Digital Learning

Children today are much more comfortable using information technology than those of previous generations. Many grow up playing video games offering strong visual and audio stimulation, instant feedback on decisions, and nonfinancial rewards for achievement such as winning competitions, accumulating points, or being able to move to the next level of a game. The popularity of such games confirms what parents and good teachers know instinctively: that children can acquire knowledge and learn new skills at seemingly phenomenal speeds when they are fully engaged in the learning experience.

Technology applied to learning, also known as digital learning or online adaptive instruction, has vast potential to transform schooling. Terry Moe and John Chubb have made a strong case that technology will cause the "creative destruction" of America's K–12 school system.[1] Either by itself or "blended" with traditional classroom teaching, digital learning is building a record of results substantially superior to traditional teaching and potentially far cheaper when used on a large scale.[2]

Digital learning stands on its own or adds great blended value because it can adapt to the capacity and speed of individual learners, provide minute-by-minute feedback on learning progress, and provide rewards suitable for individual learners. It is similar to an imaginary inexhaustible, highly skilled tutor. Even the impressive results documented later in this chapter are likely to be quickly surpassed since designers of digital courses can use billions of student responses not only to provide exemplary tutoring tailored to individual students' needs but also to continuously improve each step in the lessons.

Digital learning during childhood has the additional advantage of leading to mastery of skills, technological and other, that are necessary for further learning in subsequent grades, in college, and on the job. A survey of 300 professionals, for example, showed they spend 40 percent of their time in online communities interacting with others, and some 80 percent participate in online groups sharing information, ideas, and experiences.[3]

In this chapter we review how digital learning works and then look at three examples of its successful use: Rocketship Education, Khan Academy, and massive online open-enrollment courses (or MOOCs). We then review the scholarly research on the effects of technology on academic achievement and present best practices for removing institutional obstacles and implementing new learning technology.

Online Adaptive Instruction

Online adaptive *testing*, which was the subject of Chapter 8, becomes a part of online adaptive *instruction* when computer programs and technology measure a student's progress while also selecting the next educational steps and lessons – sometimes called the student's "playlist" – that meets the student's specific instructional needs. Instead of passively listening to other students responding to questions asked by a teacher, each student actively responds at each step in a lesson. If the student is correct, the lesson immediately proceeds to the next step much like a tutor; if incorrect, the technology quickly remediates, making sure the student does not have to struggle with more advanced steps and lessons that rely on a piece of information or skill not yet acquired or, even worse, repeat and even practice mistakes. In these ways, technology resembles a skilled tutor but at a vastly lower per-pupil cost.

Online adaptive instruction can be "blended" with classroom instruction to create "hybrid" schools such as the Rocketship Education charter schools described below.[4] Computer-based instruction can offer sounds, memorable images, and animated graphics; interpret written, typed, and spoken input such as dictation; and deliver instant feedback to student responses. Integrated data management systems can continuously update students' records on multiple devices enabling students, parents, and teachers to each view a "dashboard" presenting data in ways best suited to their needs. Students spending time in a computer lab can be supervised by older students or teacher aides, freeing teachers to spend time in smaller seminar-style meetings or one-on-one tutorial sessions with students. The result is a boost in teacher productivity as well as in student learning.

Students can use online programs inside and outside school, effectively expanding the school day and school year.[5] The Internet delivers lessons 24 hours a day, seven days a week, 365 days a year, something even the most dedicated teacher cannot do. Since programs and data are stored and retrieved from a central location, software need not be downloaded to desktop or laptop computers, allowing the use of increasingly convenient, cheap, light, and powerful devices such as tablets and smart phones. Learning can take place in school, at home, and elsewhere.

Education technology entrepreneurs are rapidly expanding the kind of adaptive software and "cloudware" available. They are producing programs for classroom management and behavior tools as well as course content. Launched in 2011, for example, ClassDojo™[6] is an online program that allows teachers to continually track and manage student behavior in class, award points for specific good behavior like attentiveness and politeness and subtract them for poor behavior such as being disruptive or not turning in homework. Teachers can choose to make students' points visible to the class throughout the day, providing greater motivation to some students to behave well.

Goalbook[7] is a similar program, this one for students with special needs. It allows all of a child's teachers and assistants to update the child's Individualized Education Plan simultaneously, if they like, keeping everyone informed about the child's progress and difficulties without requiring constant conversations and paperwork. Goalbook allows teachers to set personal learning goals for each child, such as reading a third-grade-level book or mastering the nine-times multiplication table, and to track learner progress. The system also allows for instant reports on the child's progress.

Adaptive instruction can be successful even without expert teachers. In one program, high-school students were recruited to teach reading to Head Start preschoolers in a low-income, half-minority Georgia community using a computer program called Funnix.[8] Funnix uses a step-by-step, sequential approach to teaching phonics that is highly scripted but also personalized through the computer program.[9] The high-schoolers were more successful in teaching reading than the regular teaching staff that used traditional methods. Halfway through the year, the Funnix group had reached reading levels of about a year ahead of the control group and was better at skills like naming letters, identifying the initial sounds of words, and reading words. Based on similar research, schools from California to Maryland are beginning to use the same type of instruction.

The three programs just described and the programs examined next use technology to solve problems that otherwise reduce the effectiveness of reward systems: difficult and time-consuming collection of accurate data regarding outputs; too much time between an action and a reward or penalty; goals that don't accurately reflect the learner's current interests and abilities; and reliance on rewards that haven't been proven to motivate learners. Experience demonstrates that automating achievement testing and adapting instruction to the learner's progress is enormously motivating for students as well as teachers. Digital learning solves the problems identified by Alfie Kohn and other critics of rewards. (See Chapter 1.)

Rocketship Education

Mentioned earlier, Rocketship Education charter schools provide an example of the use of online adaptive learning that appears to be economical, works for students from all backgrounds, and can be adopted on a large scale.[10] Founded in San Jose, California in 2006, Rocketship Education charter schools offer "hybrid" learning to their K–5 students, some 90 percent of whom are poor and minority. Rocketship opened its first school, Mateo Sheedy Elementary, in 2007. It has since opened six additional K–5 elementary schools serving low-income and minority students in San Jose. An eighth Rocketship school, Rocketship Southside Community Prep, opened in Milwaukee, Wisconsin in August 2013. Rocketship's founders aspire "to ultimately open regional [school] clusters in 50 cities, effectively changing the lives of over 1 million students."[11]

Rocketship students spend two hours a day in the Learning Lab, a computer lab where they work on software that teaches basic math and literacy skills.[12] Computerized instruction focuses on repetitive and drill-intensive tasks such as arithmetic and spelling and gives teachers up-to-the-minute assessments of each student, which they then use to guide one-on-one and small group sessions with students during the rest of the school day. Rocketship says the time its students spend in the computer lab allows the company to hire between five and six fewer teachers in a school, about 25 percent of the total teaching staff, generating an annual savings of about $500,000.[13] Some of the savings is used for higher pay for teachers and to pay for the aides who act as coaches in the computer labs, but more importantly the savings make the model financially sustainable and scalable since charter schools typically receive per-pupil stipends that are less than what traditional public schools spend. In 2013, Rocketship Education announced plans to modify its system by placing teachers in addition to aides in the Learning Labs, with one teacher for each group of 90 students.[14]

Data from the California Department of Education confirm the success of the Rocketship model. In 2012, Rocketship Mateo Sheedy Elementary, the first of the Rocketship schools to open, scored 924 on California's Academic Performance Index (API), well above the state average of 815.[15] The five Rocketship schools enrolling students at the time the state tests were administered achieved an overall performance of 855, despite the lower socioeconomic status of their students.

Rocketship Education Charter Schools **2012 Performance on California Academic Performance Index**	
Rocketship Los Sueños	793
Rocketship Discovery Prep	805
California Statewide Average	815
Rocketship Sí Se Puede Academy	861
Rocketship Overall Average	855
Rocketship Mosaic Academy	872
Rocketship Mateo Sheedy Elementary	924
Source: Rocketship Education, "Academic Performance," http://www.rsed.org/about/Academic-Performance.cfm, viewed on June 13, 2013.	

"School Quality Snapshots," a website maintained by the California Department of Education, also confirms the Rocketship schools' high performance.[16] On the math portion of the 2011–12 California Standards Test, for example, 80 percent of Rocketship students scored Proficient or Advanced, on par with the ten most affluent school districts in California.

In 2011, SRI International, a nonprofit research and development organization, conducted a 16-week study of Rocketship's use of DreamBox

Learning, an online math tool. Students in kindergarten and first grade used the program. The study found, "Rocketship students who received additional online math instruction through the DreamBox Learning program scored substantially higher on an independent mathematics test than similar students who did not receive the additional online instruction time. For the average student, these gains would be equivalent to progressing 5.5 points in percentile ranking (e.g. from 50 percent to 55.5 percent) in just 16 weeks."[17] If that performance enhancement were continued over the course of a student's entire K–12 career, the difference in academic standing at graduation would be huge.

"The SRI study confirms Rocketship's core belief that adaptive, online learning positively impacts students' overall academic achievement," said Chief Schools Officer Aylon Samouha. "The use of highly effective, cost-efficient individualized instructional programs like DreamBox Learning is allowing Rocketship to realize its mission of closing the achievement gap."[18]

While many charter schools now incorporate adaptive instruction into the school day, Rocketship has concentrated on creating a business model that will enable it to produce hundreds of schools each generating superior results at a lower per-pupil cost than public schools. This requires designing schools that do not rely on charity or exceptional leaders or teachers willing to work 70 hours a week or longer and do everything from raising funds and recruiting and managing staff to providing after-school counseling to students.

Khan Academy

Khan Academy is not a school, yet more than 200 million students have taken one or more of the lessons it offers. Hosting a free online library of more than 3,300 videos that are now being used by charter and traditional schools across the country and around the world, Khan Academy demonstrates how technology can transform education through adaptive instruction and the enormous reach of the Internet.

Khan Academy started in 2004 when Salman Khan started filming himself giving short lectures on math in a closet in his home and posting them on the Internet. Khan noticed the growing popularity of his videos and the short quizzes he wrote for each one and, with the help of philanthropists such as Bill Gates, was soon able to dramatically ramp up the number of videos and pay technical experts to make them compatible with adaptive testing and instruction programs.

How does Khan Academy work? Let's take learning math as an example. Students first watch free ten-minute videos on core math concepts starting at the beginning with addition, subtraction, and the idea of numbers. They then take tests to determine how well they have understood the material. Online adaptive tests track the errors the students make and cue up the next set of videos and concepts to target the students' strengths and weaknesses. As students progress, they earn badges and points – familiar examples of rewards described throughout this book – for concepts they have mastered.

By 2012, Khan Academy was providing free access to more than 3,300 free micro-lectures, many interactive, on mathematics, physics, chemistry, organic chemistry, biology, astronomy, cosmology, American civics, art history, finance, economics, computer science, and health care and medicine.[19] A growing number of schools, now numbering in the thousands, use this online instructional library to supplement regular courses by viewing the videos in class or assigning them as homework. Khan also has expanded to offer free online college-level courses.

An online library of educational videos, even when accompanied by adaptive testing and instruction, is not a complete solution to what ails K–12 education in America. Like other activities in a computer lab, it provides a component of a blended model where teachers can help young learners keep track of time, answer questions, provide guidance, and offer encouragement. But streaming video to 100 or more computer workstations requires substantial bandwidth, which can be expensive or not available in some schools. And the Khan Academy library has not yet been completely built out, leaving gaps in some subjects and not much depth to some of the quizzes.

What is so surprising about Khan Academy isn't that it has faults and limitations, but that something like it exists at all. It came out of nowhere less than a decade ago and is now part of the educational experiences of millions of students in the U.S. and millions more around the world. The videos and tests it makes available for free are genuinely revolutionizing learning for students of all ages and backgrounds, from the children of Bill Gates (and Gates himself, who reported using Khan videos to brush up on his math skills) to the most disadvantaged children in inner cities. It does this for a tiny per-pupil cost. The success of Khan Academy shows that, despite the resistance of the public education establishment to changes to its delivery model, a single person has the power to go around that inertia and dramatically change the educational opportunities for millions of children by coming up with an innovative idea, using modern technology to implement that idea quickly and inexpensively, and then using the Internet to freely publish that idea for education-hungry children around the world.

Massive Online Open-Enrollment Courses (MOOCs)

In 2011, Stanford University professor Sebastian Thrun taught 160,000 students a course on artificial intelligence using uploaded videos of himself lecturing and drawing diagrams on a napkin.[20] He had opened the class to anyone in the world and placed all the assignments and tests online for anyone to take. Students located all around the world took the course. More students from Lithuania enrolled in his class than were enrolled in Stanford. Some students wrote him to explain that they lived in war-torn countries like Afghanistan and had to dodge flak to search for an Internet connection to complete their assignments.

Of that first class, 23,000 students finished the course and 248 never scored a single wrong answer on any of the class tests. Not one of those 248 students attended Stanford. Thrun's physical class of 200 students at Stanford dwindled until only about 30 students attended class regularly. The rest preferred to watch his video lecture online because they felt the online instruction was more intimate and helped them learn better. Thrun is now developing a free online university following a similar pattern. He plans to offer a master's degree for $100, in contrast to a typical current cost of around $45,000.[21]

Thrun's course and efforts are part of a global phenomenon called massive online open-enrollment courses, or MOOCs. Thrun launched Udacity in January 2012 and two of his colleagues launched Coursera three months later. Udacity's most popular course, on computer science, has enrolled more than 270,000 students. Some 74 universities around the world have signed up to provide courses.[22] The courses feature some of the world's most renowned experts delivering lectures and participating in online conversations with millions of students who otherwise would never have the opportunity to attend college, much less take courses taught by such eminent scholars. Adaptive testing and instruction technologies work as well as part of MOOCs as they do for Khan Academy and the blended classrooms of Rocketship and other charter schools, freeing lecturers from the drudgery of repeating lectures and answering predictable questions while greatly accelerating students' learning. Social networking tools such as online discussion forums can create the sense of community and connectivity that brick-and-mortar campuses promise but don't always deliver.

MOOCs seem to be taking off in higher education because private and public universities genuinely compete for students and tuition and their faculties are largely non-union and so tend not to organize to oppose labor-saving technologies.[23] Lack of competition and the presence of strong teachers unions pose obstacles to their adoption at the K–12 level, but as these barriers are overcome, success should be even greater than in higher education due to the much larger size of the market and the subject matter being simpler. The number of lessons for K–12 education in English, mathematics, science, civics, major foreign languages, art, music, and perhaps a few other subjects would be less than the thousands of specialized courses universities provide.

If MOOCs can drive down the cost of a two-year college masters degree from $45,000 to $100, what could it do for K–12 schooling? Yes, K–12 schools perform a custodial function that colleges do not, so there may be continuing demand for "real" schools. But technological innovations such as the Khan Academy and MOOCs are genuinely transformational, pointing to an educational model that is fundamentally different from today's K–12 classroom.

Digital Learning and Achievement

Online adaptive instruction can provide in one package the goals, activities, tests, and incentives needed to accelerate student learning. Students receive feedback as they move through a set of activities that the program customizes to their individual abilities. Many programs utilize algorithms grounded in psychological research on common errors students have made in face-to-face settings. Such research makes it possible to offer detailed cues for what to do next and prompt the user to move on to more difficult levels or repeat a lesson perhaps from another perspective when appropriate.

A meta-analysis of 20 years of research conducted by Mickey Shachar and Yoram Neumann in 2010 showed adaptive online education programs on average provide better learning results than traditionally taught classes.[24] As the table on the following page demonstrates, most studies across various time periods showed superior results for the online programs. While 70 percent of all studies found online classes to be superior, 84 percent of studies published after 2002 found online superiority, suggesting (as we would expect) that online performance is improving over time.

Studies after 2002 showed not only superiority but a very large average additional effect of +0.403, corresponding roughly to what is learned in four-tenths of a school year, which means the typical online education student exceeds 66 percent of traditionally taught students. Many of the studies in Shachar and Neumann's analysis were conducted before or shortly after the Internet became such a widespread means of communicating across the world. Today's online programs are significantly superior to those of five years ago and getting even better, and more students, homes, and schools have the bandwidth to access the most advanced forms of online instruction.

Meta-Analysis of Online Education Effects			
Implementation Period	Number of Studies	Average Effect Size	Percentage Above Control Group Average
1991–1998	38	.266	61%
1999–2000	33	.068	53%
2001–2002	29	.310	62%
2003–2009	25	.403	66%

Note: The data in this table are derived from Mickey Shachar and Yoram Neumann, "Twenty Years of Research on the Academic Performance Differences Between Traditional and Distance Learning: Summative Meta-Analysis and Trend Examination," MERLOT Journal of Online Learning and Teaching 6, no. 2 (June 2010): 318–34. The effect sizes are averaged across all studies conducted in the period indicated. The final column is the percentage of traditional students exceeded in achievement by online students.

Most of the studies reviewed by Shachar and Neumann reported the effects of a single unit or at most a year of study. If these effects could be achieved each year over a student's K–12 career, the result would be transformational. American students would easily rank first rather than as low as 32nd in international achievement surveys. Many, moreover, would be ready for college-level work after as little as nine years of schooling rather than the usual 12.

Another meta-analysis of online learning studies conducted for the U.S. Department of Education and published in 2010 provides further evidence of the superiority of digital learning, though its findings were couched in cautionary language.[25] The researchers found 50 experimental or controlled quasi-experimental studies comparing the learning effects of online versus face-to-face instruction, including only five published studies involving K–12 students that met their meta-analysis criteria. Students who engaged in only online learning exceeded the achievement outcomes of students receiving only traditional instruction with an average effect size of +0.20. Students in blended learning environments benefitted from an average effect of +0.35. Earlier reviews of distance education also showed substantial effects.[26]

While there are obstacles to the spread of digital learning, cost is not one of them. The per-pupil costs of online schooling, which requires fewer teachers, have only recently been compared to that of traditional classroom instruction. According to a study by the Thomas B. Fordham Institute, full online learning on average costs about $4,300 annually less than traditional schooling while the blended model saves about $1,100 per student per year.[27] These cost savings are likely to increase over time as the technology improves and as educators gain experience in its use. Requiring nine rather than 12 years of schooling would reduce costs substantially more.

Best Practices
Digital learning is spreading quickly as parents, students, and educators recognize its transformational potential. Some obstacles need to be overcome such as certification requirements that block entry into the teaching profession by talented and motivated individuals, seat-time and class-size requirements that make school schedules rigid and unable to accommodate computer lab sessions, and opposition from teachers unions.[28] A rapidly growing community of educators with experience using digital learning tools and a literature describing best practices are available to reformers who want to accelerate this progress.

The Digital Learning Council, a nonprofit organization launched in 2010 to integrate current and future technological innovations into public education, has produced a series of publications (all of them available online) to help parents, educators, and policymakers find and use the best practices for digital learning. The council has proposed "10 Elements of High Quality Digital Learning," which it describes as "actions that need to be taken by lawmakers and policymakers to foster a high-quality, customized education for all students. This includes technology-enhanced learning in traditional schools, online and virtual learning, and blended learning that combines online and onsite learning."[29] Those actions appear in the table on page 145.

In 2011, the American Legislative Exchange Council (ALEC), a respected membership organization for state legislators, adopted a model resolution endorsing the "ten elements" approach.[30] In 2012, ALEC created and endorsed model legislation, the Statewide Online Education Act, that provides a detailed template for states to follow to remove roadblocks to expanding digital learning.[31] The National Conference of State Legislatures (NCSL), another organization of state legislators, also has endorsed expanding the use of digital learning and provides case studies of its successful implementation.[32]

An implementation guide for blended learning produced by the Digital Learning Council recommends state government policies that support full- and part-time access to online learning by eliminating seat-time requirements, providing end-of-course tests on demand, making funding portable (following students to the schools or colleges that offer online courses), shifting from traditional textbooks to digital instructional materials, and supporting expanded broadband access for schools.[33] At the school level, the authors stress that simply adding computers to classrooms doesn't accelerate learning unless those computers "change instructional practices, schedules, relationships, and resource allocations."[34]

The Clayton Christensen Institute for Disruptive Innovation, formerly the Innosight Institute, is another good source of best practices.[35] The nonprofit think tank was founded by Harvard professor Clayton M. Christensen, author of the 2008 best-seller *Disrupting Class: How Disruptive Innovation Will Change the Way the World Learns*. The organization conducts original research on the cutting edge of digital learning, consults with elected officials, and provides speakers for public events. Researchers affiliated with the organization have created a "blended-learning taxonomy" that distinguishes among the various ways of blending digital learning with traditional schooling, such as Station

Rotation, Lab Rotation, Flipped Classroom, Flex, A La Carte, Enriched Virtual, and Individual Rotation models.[36]

Ten Elements of High-Quality Digital Learning

1. *Student Eligibility*: All students are digital learners.

2. *Student Access*: All students have access to high-quality digital learning.

3. *Personalized Learning*: All students can use digital learning to customize their education.

4. *Advancement*: All students progress based on demonstrated competency.

5. *Quality Content*: Digital content and courses are high quality.

6. *Quality Instruction*: Digital instruction is high quality.

7. *Quality Choices*: All students have access to multiple high-quality digital providers.

8. *Assessment and Accountability*: Student learning is the metric for evaluating the quality of content and instruction.

9. *Funding*: Funding creates incentives for performance, options and innovation.

10. *Delivery*: Infrastructure supports digital learning.

Source: Digital Learning Council, "Ten Elements of High Quality Digital Learning," http://www.digitallearningnow.com/10elements/, viewed on June 23, 2013. See source for original phrasing of these points.

Conclusion

Digital learning – the combination of online adaptive testing and instruction made possible by new technologies, software, and the Internet – is beginning to transform K–12 education. It accelerates learning for a number of reasons, but an important one is because it makes rewards for learning more accurate, timely, and attuned to the interests and abilities of students. It promises to deliver the "creative destruction" required to substantially improve America's failing elementary and high-school system.

ClassDojo, Goalbook, and Funnix are three examples of the rapidly growing number of software programs available to educators to bring digital learning into the classroom. Rocketship Education, Khan Academy, Coursera, and Udacity illustrate the variety of new institutions that are using digital learning to transform traditional teaching methods. Given the pace at which software is improving and institutions are evolving, these examples may seem out-of-date in a few years.

Research described in this chapter shows substantial positive achievement effects of online education in pre-Internet days and larger effects in recent years. More advanced technologies used on a much wider scale promise even larger achievement effects, lower costs, and a greater variety of incentives, curricula, and teaching methods from which parents, students, and educators can choose. Obstacles in the path to increased use of digital learning can be removed by parents and policymakers working together to adopt the policies recommended by pioneering leaders in the field, the Digital Learning Council, and other groups supporting this disruptive innovation likely leading to far more effective education.

Notes

1. Terry M. Moe and John E. Chubb, *Liberating Learning: Technology, Politics, and the Future of American Education* (San Francisco, CA: Jossey-Bass, Wiley, 2009). See also Clayton Christensen, Curtis W. Johnson, and Michael B. Horn, *Disrupting Class: How Disruptive Innovation Will Change the Way the World Learns* (New York, NY: McGraw-Hill, 2008).

2. For an early but still impressive compilation of research see D.P. Ely and Tjeerd Plomp, eds., *International Encyclopedia of Educational Technology, 2nd edition* (London: Emerald Group Publishing, 1996).

3. Jaan Valsiner and Rene van der Veer, *The Social Mind* (New York, NY: Cambridge University Press, 2000).

4. Michael B. Horn and Heather Staker, *The Rise of K–12 Blended Learning*, Innosight Institute, January 2011, http://www.innosightinstitute.org/innosight/wp-content/uploads/2011/01/The-Rise-of-K-12-Blended-Learning.pdf.

5. Jenny Brown, "When Is a System an Integrated Learning System?" in Jean D.M. Underwood and Jenny Brown, eds., *Integrated Learning Systems: Potential into Practice* (London: Heinemann, 1997).

6. See www.classdojo.com.

7. See http://goalbookapp.com.

8. Jean Stockard, "Promoting Early Literacy of Preschool Children," *Technical Report 2009-01*, National Institute for Direct Instruction, March 2009, http://www.funnix.com/funnix2006/PDFs/ FUNNIX-Research-Stockard-09.pdf.

9. See www.funnix.com.

10. Jonathan Schorr and Debora McGriff, "Future Schools," *Education Next* 11, no. 3 (Summer 2011). See also Laura Vanderkam, *Blended Learning: A Wise Giver's Guide to Supporting Tech-assisted Teaching* (Washington, DC: Philanthropy Roundtable, 2013), pp. 34–41.

11. Rocketship Education, "Our Story," http://www.rsed.org/about/Our-Story.cfm.

12. Ben DeGrow, "California Charter 'Rockets' to Hybrid Learning Success," *School Reform News*, March 24, 2010, http://news.heartland.org/newspaper-article/2010/03/24/california-charter-rockets-hybrid-learning-success.

13. John Fensterwald, "Learning Labs 101," *Scholastic*, http://www.scholastic.com/browse/article.jsp?id=3757077.

14. Laura Vanderkam, *supra* note 10, p. 37.

15. Rocketship Education, "Academic Performance," http://www.rsed.org/about/Academic-Performance.cfm, viewed on June 13, 2013.

16. California Department of Education, *School Quality Snapshot, 2011–2012*, http://www6.cde.ca.gov/schoolqualitysnapshot/. Enter "Rocketship" and then select the individual schools from the pull-down menu.

17. SRI International, "SRI Study: Rocketship Students Experience Stronger Math Gains with More Online Instruction," news release, August 2, 2011, http://www.sri.com/newsroom/press-releases/sri-study-rocketship-students-experience-stronger-math-gains-more-online-i-0.

18. *Ibid.*

19. Khan Academy, http://www.khanacademy.org/.

20. Sebastian Thrun, "University 2.0," remarks at the Digital Life Design Conference, Munich, Germany, January 23, 2012, http://new.livestream.com/accounts/50648/events/698/videos/112950.

21. Jacqueline Spiegel, "On Statistics and Open Education: A Brief Chat with Sebastian Thrun," *I Programmer*, June 15, 2012, http://www.i-programmer.info/professional-programmer/accreditation/4365-on-stat-class-udacity-and-open-ed-a-brief-chat-with-sebastian-thrun-.html.

22. M. Mitchell Waldrop, "Campus 2.0," *Nature* 495 (March 14, 2013): 161.

23. Nevertheless, college professors are attempting to organize to oppose MOOCs. See Steve Kolowich, "Faculty Backlash Grows Against Online Partnerships," *The Chronicle of Higher Education*, May 6, 2013, http://chronicle.com/article/Faculty-Backlash-Grows-Against/139049/.

24. Mickey Shachar and Yoram Neumann, "Twenty Years of Research on the Academic Performance Differences Between Traditional and Distance Learning: Summative Meta-Analysis and Trend Examination," *MERLOT Journal of Online Learning and Teaching* 6, no. 2 (June 2010): 318–34.

25. Barbara Means, Yukie Toyama, Robert Murphy, Marianne Bakia, and Karla Jones, "Evaluation of Evidence-Based Practices in Online Learning: A Meta-Analysis and Review of Online Learning Studies," U.S. Department of Education, Office of Planning, Evaluation and Policy Development, Policy and Program Studies Service, September 2010.

26. Judy M. Parr and Irene Fung, *A Review of the Literature on Computer-Assisted Learning, Particularly Integrated Learning Systems, and Outcomes with Respect to Literacy and Numeracy* (Wellington, NZ: Auckland Uniservices Unlimited, 2000).

27. Tamara Butler Battaglino, Matt Haldeman, and Eleanor Laurans, "The Costs of Online Learning," in Chester E. Finn, Jr. and Daniela R. Fairchild, eds., *Education Reform for the Digital Era* (Washington, DC: Thomas B. Fordham Institute, 2012), pp. 55–76.

28. Chester E. Finn, Jr. and Daniella R. Fairchild, "Overcoming the Obstacles to Digital Learning"; Paul T. Hill, "School Finance in the Digital-Learning Era"; and John E. Chubb, "Overcoming the Governance Challenge in K–12 Online Learning," all in Chester E. Finn, Jr. and Daniela R. Fairchild, eds., *ibid.*, pp. 1–11, 77–98, and 99–134.

29. Digital Learning Council, "Ten Elements of High Quality Digital Learning," http://www.digitallearningnow.com/10elements/, viewed on June 23, 2013.

30. American Legislative Exchange Council, "Resolution Adopting the 10 Elements of High Quality Digital Learning," http://www.alec.org/model-legislation/resolution-adopting-the-10-elements-of-high-quali ty-digital-learning-for-k-12/, viewed on June 23, 2013.

31. American Legislative Exchange Council, "Statewide Online Education Act," http://www.alec.org/model-legislation/statewide-online-education-act/, viewed on June 23, 2013.

32. Sunny Deyé, "K–12 Online Learning Options," National Conference of State Legislatures, *Legisbriefs* 21, no. 16 (April 2013).

33. John Bailey, Scott Ellis, Carri Schneider, and Tom Vander Ark, "Blended Learning Implementation Guide," *Digital Learning Now*, p. 6, http://www.digitallearningnow.com/wp-content/uploads/2013/02/DLNSmartSeries-BL-p aper_2012-02-05a.pdf.

34. *Ibid.*

35. http://www.christenseninstitute.org/education/.

36. Clayton M. Christensen, Michael B. Horn, and Heather Staker, "Is K–12 Blended Learning Disruptive? An Introduction of the Theory of Hybrids," Clayton Christensen Institute, May 2013, http://www.christenseninstitute.org/wp-content/uploads/2013/05/ Is-K-12-Blended-Learning-Disruptive.pdf.

11

Rewards and School Choice

Kindergarten through 12th grade public education in the United States relies too much on intrinsic motivation and not enough on extrinsic motivation. Competition and consumer choice, which create rewards for greater effort and achievement in much of American life, are highly constrained or absent in K–12 public schools. Attaching student rewards to tests and performance-based compensation for teachers can only partly make up for this dysfunctional organization.

The reform most likely to transform the nation's schools is allowing them the flexibility to specialize and strive for excellence as they define it, and to give parents the freedom to choose, without financial penalties, the schools best suited for their children. This combination of school flexibility and portable funding – sometimes called weighted student funding or "backpack funding" since the student carries his or her education funds directly to the parents' chosen school – is what we mean by school choice.

School choice programs were shown in Chapter 3 to significantly improve student academic achievement, increase parental satisfaction, and generate other benefits. Expanding school choice, however, is opposed by teachers unions and many "progressive" educators. For example, Margaret Diane LeCompte and Anthony Gary Dworkin dismiss school choice as "private solutions to a public problem" that "violate deeply held American cultural ethics."[1] This chapter explains why that view is wrong.

School choice creates incentives that change the behavior of students, parents, teachers, and administrators. It solves the problems, presented in Chapters 4 and 8, of how to set educational goals and fairly use objective tests for achievement in a diverse democratic society. Four kinds of school choice show particular promise: charter schools, the parent trigger, vouchers (or scholarships), and education savings accounts. We will describe successful examples of each of these choice programs and then present best practices for school reformers to launch or expand them in their cities and states.

A State of Emergency

If students attending public schools in the United States were generally achieving at high levels, it might be unnecessary to propose that those schools be fundamentally changed – transformed – rather than merely reformed. Perhaps they could be made better by adopting more of the rewards we've shown to be highly effective inside and outside schools. Perhaps they would just need to change the tests they administer, or how they pay teachers, or add computers to more classrooms. Regrettably, this is not the situation we face. Public education in the U.S. is in a state of emergency and needs the kind of fundamental change that only school choice can deliver.

In 1983 the National Commission on Excellence in Education, a blue-ribbon panel appointed by President Ronald Reagan, warned in its report *A Nation at Risk* that "the educational foundations of our society are presently being eroded by a rising tide of mediocrity that threatens our very future as a Nation and a people."[2] "If an unfriendly foreign power had attempted to impose on America the mediocre educational performance that exists today," its authors declared, "we might well have viewed it as an act of war."[3]

This is not a partisan sentiment. Bruce Maclaury, president of the liberal Brookings Institution, wrote in 1990,[4]

> By most accounts, the American education system is not working well. Children appear to be learning less in school today than they did a generation ago. Some 25 percent of the nation's high school students drop out before graduating, and in large cities – whose poor and minority children desperately need quality education – the figure can climb to 50 percent. On math and science achievement tests, American teenagers trail students from other nations – a pattern with alarming implications for America's ability to compete in the world economy.

Even progressives agree. "[E]ducation in the United States is in a virtual state of emergency," wrote LeCompte and Dworkin in 1991.[5] "We feel that the situation many American children experience in their homes and neighborhoods and the conditions that confront their future are devastating. Furthermore, the conditions under which teachers are expected to teach and children are expected to learn are catastrophic."[6]

During the 40 years since publication of *A Nation at Risk* a host of costly reforms has been attempted, among them changing teacher training and certification, curriculum, class size, and school size; centralizing and decentralizing administration; setting high academic standards, linking and unlinking them to curriculum, and then abandoning and attempting to resurrect the same; discouraging or banning such common rewards as grades and praise; and much more. Through it all, the key measures of academic achievement in the U.S. have remained stubbornly poor.[7]

Only 40 percent of U.S. fourth-graders and 35 percent of eighth-graders scored "proficient" or better in mathematics on the 2011 National Assessment of Educational Progress (NAEP), and only 34 percent of fourth- and eighth-graders were proficient in reading.[8] Only 32 percent of eighth-graders were proficient or better in science.[9] There is some evidence that even these numbers overstate student achievement because states that report the most progress exclude high numbers of students from groups that often bring scores down, including learning-disabled students and English Language Learners (ELL).[10]

In 2009, the scores of U.S. 15-year-olds on international assessment tests for reading and science literacy were "not measurably different from the OECD [Organization for Economic Cooperation and Development] average" and were below the OECD average for mathematics literacy.[11] U.S. students used to outperform their counterparts in other developed countries.

The U.S. high-school graduation rate for 2010–11 was only 75.5 percent, indicating that one in four students who make it to high school drops out before graduating.[12] Some 1,550 public high schools reported dropout rates of 60 percent or more.[13]

The problem is not a lack of spending. Real per-pupil spending (adjusted for inflation) rose 23.5 percent between 1994 and 2004 and more than doubled from 1970 to 2005.[14] Research by dozens of scholars has found no consistent relationship between higher spending and improvement in academic achievement.[15] The problem is declining productivity – the ratio of outputs to inputs. American school productivity fell by between 55 and 73 percent between 1970–71 and 1998–99, depending on the skill and age cohort tested.[16] If schools today were only as productive as they were in 1970–71, the average 17-year-old would have a score that fewer than 5 percent of 17-year-olds currently attain.[17]

The falling productivity of government schools can be traced to three developments inside the public school establishment. The first is growth of a vast bureaucracy of nonteaching personnel. Government schools in the United States report a higher ratio of nonteaching personnel to teachers than government schools in any other developed country.[18] In 2005, teachers comprised just 51.2 percent of all the staff employed by public elementary and secondary school systems in the U.S.[19]

The second trend is the fall in average class size. The number of teachers rose significantly faster than school enrollment after 1970, although not as rapidly as nonteaching personnel. The ratio of students to teachers in public schools fell from 17.6:1 in 1987 to 15.4:1 in 2007, a decrease of 12.5 percent.[20] The third reason for the low productivity of government schools is a dropout rate that has not fallen despite large increases in spending and personnel. Students who drop out before graduating increase the cost per graduated, or finished, student.

This record of failure suggests the problem facing public schools is deeper than many reformers think. It is time to raise questions about the fundamental organization of public schools.

School Choice and Incentives

Government control of schools is often justified by appeals to the special role schools play in democratic societies, and indeed this is a concern that cannot be dismissed. But that control need not be exercised as it is today in American public K–12 education. Having government agencies own school facilities, hire teachers, approve curriculum, set standards, finance operations exclusively through tax dollars, and systemically discourage competition among public schools and between public and private schools has been a recipe for dysfunction rather than success. This model, copied from the Prussian system of compulsory state-funded schools in the early nineteenth century, has all the disadvantages of a monopoly and none of the virtues of a democracy or market economy.[21]

An alternative model is for government to encourage or require universal free education up to or through high school while also recognizing the right of parents to have their children educated in privately organized schools, whether nonprofit or for-profit, without financial penalties. Giving parents the power to choose private schools, including religious schools, for their children is the rule rather than the exception among advanced democracies, which may help explain why U.S. students perform poorly compared to students in other countries.[22]

School choice creates incentives and opportunities that can accelerate student achievement. For children, "choice gives students a reason for going to a school. When attending a particular school by choice, students are less likely to see themselves as draftees 'biding their time' until graduation; they tend to see more purpose in going to school. This purposefulness (or a lack of it) can be felt in a school's halls and classrooms; it can be seen on the faces of students and teachers."[23]

Parents also enthusiastically embrace school choice programs. A recent survey found that 66 percent of mothers with school-age children "support vouchers for all students to obtain the best education possible. Mothers with school-age children also have more confidence in private school settings than in traditional public schools."[24] Polls by Gallup, Public Agenda, and political scientist Terry M. Moe find similar levels of support.[25]

Parents respond to school choice by becoming more involved in their children's education, which is strongly correlated with improved academic success.[26] Parents who are empowered by school choice know their concerns are being taken seriously and are welcome to participate in their schools' management. They respond by becoming educational partners with teachers and administrators. The power to choose among competing schools gives parents much greater influence over the schools their children attend than merely being one of many voters casting votes in elections for school board members. School choice allows parents to change the schools their children attend without having to move to a different community or pay twice for their children's tuition, once through state and local property taxes and again when paying tuition at a private school.

At the school level, school administrators behave differently when they face tough competition for students and funding from nearby schools.[27] Pressure to hold down costs would exist if schools had to compete for students and tuition, but such competition is weak or entirely absent because the current system assigns students to schools in their neighborhoods and public funds go largely to public schools with similar organizations and curricula.

School choice allows school boards and principals to focus on establishing clarity and consensus about school goals and incentives, which is the key to turning around failing schools.[28] Houston recently accomplished this with nine of its worst public schools.[29] The school district replaced every principal in these schools, nearly one-third of other school-level administrators, and more than half of the schools' teachers. To fill their places, the district hired educators "who possessed the values and beliefs consistent with an achievement-driven mantra and, wherever possible, a demonstrated record of achievement."[30] In one year, students in these schools made "dramatic" mathematics and reading achievement gains similar to students in high-quality charter schools.

In the current system, much of the control and decision-making regarding individual schools is exercised at the state and district levels, which issue top-down edicts and rules in an attempt to achieve clarity and consensus. However, this approach is doomed to failure. Bureaucracies rely on restricting the options and choices of people at the bottom of hierarchies in order to compel them to act in certain ways despite incentives and their desires to act otherwise.[31] This leads to what has been called "Campbell's law of performance measurement": "The more any quantitative social indicator is used for social decision-making, the more subject it will be to corruption pressures and the more apt it will be to distort and corrupt the social processes it is intended to monitor."[32]

Progressive educators recognize this problem even as they refuse to embrace its solution. LeCompte and Dworkin write, "One of the real problems with school reform is implementation. Reformers tend to forget that all of the changes, whether curricular, organizational, or psychosocial, will have to be implemented with virtually the same instructional and administrative staff that existed pre-reform. ... Finally, reforms founder because of organizational inertia and resistance. Schools often greet reform initiatives with a 'circle the wagons' mentality impervious to change initiatives."[33]

Successful reforms in education give schools incentives to innovate rather than mandate single top-down solutions. Educators are allowed to focus on building consensus, discovering what resources or policies are needed, and then adopting them.[34] Teachers are allowed to find solutions through trial and error rather than being told to act as cogs in a grand scheme set forth by others remote from their classrooms. This process is sometimes called "searching" to contrast it with "planning."[35] School choice programs create an environment in which searching can replace planning.

Solving the Goal-Setting Problem

In Chapter 4 we described the nation's long history of delegating responsibility for regulating schools to state and local governments and recognizing the primacy of parents' rights over the education of their children. School choice represents one possible solution to the goal-setting problem by creating an environment in which parents and teachers are free to work together to develop the goals most suitable for each child.

The case for making parents the primary goal-setters in K–12 education is a strong one. Parents spend the most time with children and know their needs, interests, and talents best. They have a personal financial interest in seeing their children become productive adults and be successful in raising families of their own. They have a constitutional right to exercise control over their children's education. The way to involve parents in goal-setting is for state and local governments to allow schools the flexibility they need to meet the demands of parents while simultaneously giving parents the freedom to choose, without financial penalty, the schools they believe are best for their children.

Critics of school choice warn, as has Amitai Etzioni, a prominent sociologist, "there are dangers in the simplistic introduction of competition into areas of human services. In these areas the consumer's knowledge is usually limited; it is more difficult for parents to evaluate education than, say, a can of beans."[36] But no one claims choosing the best school for a child is as easy as choosing "a can of beans." Limited knowledge can be overcome by experience, producer reputations, guarantees and warranties, and personal and public sources of information. Writing back in 1978, John Coons and Stephen Sugarman pointed out, "the question is not whether the judgment of the isolated and unassisted family is superior to the professional cadre of a school or a district. It is rather, when all available knowledge, personal and professional, about the particular school is assembled, to whom shall society commit the final choice."[37]

Despite the problem of information asymmetry, consumers are routinely trusted to make decisions with major implications for their family's safety and well-being, often with professional or peer advice. We choose among competing producers for housing, food, and medicine even though few of us are licensed architects, nutritionists, or pharmacists.

Research shows that when parents are allowed to choose the schools their children attend – such as when charter schools compete with conventional public schools or when public schools compete with one another through open enrollment programs – they make careful and informed decisions.[38] Surveys show parents rate schools largely the same as experts do, and most parents choose schools on the basis of their perceived academic quality.[39] For example, a poll of New York City parents seeking privately funded scholarships to attend Catholic schools revealed the first concern of 85 percent of the parents was academic quality, while only 38 percent cited religious instruction as a significant attraction.[40] Another survey showed 81 percent of parents approved of high-stakes testing for grade promotion and 85 percent approved of expecting high-school students to pass a tough exit exam before graduating.[41] The research summarized at the end of Chapter 3 on the positive effects of choice on student academic achievement also confirms that parents choose wisely.

Evidence and experience have persuaded state policymakers to expand the ability of parents to choose the schools their children attend. In the sections that follow we describe four very different and yet successful programs that expand parental choice in education.

Charter Schools: Knowledge Is Power Program (KIPP)

Most states now offer limited school flexibility and parental choice in the form of public schools that operate on charters issued by a local school district or in some cases a different chartering entity. The charter says the school will receive a certain amount of funding per student as long as it achieves specific outputs and complies with operating standards set forth in the agreement. Students are not assigned to charter schools but instead attend only if their parents or guardians choose the school. In return for giving up the security of guaranteed enrollments and annual budgets, charter schools are exempted from various rules and regulations such as minimum class sizes, mandated curriculum, and collective bargaining agreements.

Forty-two states and the District of Columbia have enacted charter school laws.[42] Approximately 1.6 million students attended charter schools in 2010, about 3 percent of all school-age children.[43] Because charter schools are heavily concentrated in low-income neighborhoods and big cities, determining their success relative to traditional public schools can be difficult and controversial.[44] However, the best research on the subject – by Caroline M. Hoxby,[45] Bryan C. Hassel,[46] and Hoxby and Jonah E.

Rockoff[47] – shows convincing evidence of superior performance by charter schools.[48] Importantly, randomized assignment studies – the "gold standard" for social science research – show charter schools have a positive effect on achievement, though these studies tend to be small-scale.[49]

As discussed in Chapter 7, among the most successful charter school networks is the Knowledge Is Power Program (KIPP), a nationwide collection of open-enrollment middle schools commonly located in urban and poor communities. KIPP was founded in Houston, Texas in 1994 and has grown to 125 schools serving more than 41,000 students in 20 states and Washington, DC. Ninety-five percent of students enrolled in KIPP schools are minorities and more than 80 percent qualify for the federal free and reduced-price meals program for children from families in poverty.[50]

KIPP schools identify five "operating principles" that distinguish their approach from other schools: clearly defined and measurable high expectations for academic achievement and conduct; parents and the faculty choose to be part of a KIPP school ("no one is assigned or forced to attend a KIPP school"); an extended school day, week, and year; principals who are empowered to lead their schools by having control over their school budget and personnel; and a tight focus on high student performance on standardized tests and other objective measures.[51]

All five of these principles track what research shows to be the strategies of high-performing schools.[52] Without the flexibility that charter school status provides, KIPP schools would not be able to adopt these policies, and without the public funding that follows low-income students to KIPP schools, the schools would be unable to compete with free public schools or serve disadvantaged communities. Public schools in districts where KIPP operates obviously could model some of their schools on the KIPP approach but, significantly, they have not done so. Thus, without KIPP, KIPP students would still be sitting in schools that are stubbornly unresponsive to their educational needs.

KIPP teachers, parents, and students must sign agreements, called the "KIPP Commitment to Excellence," spelling out in detail their obligations to the school.[53] For example, teachers agree to arrive at the school on weekdays by 7:15 a.m. and leave no earlier than 5:00 p.m. Monday – Thursday and 4:00 p.m. on Fridays; to teach at KIPP during the summer; to "always make ourselves available to students and parents, and address any concerns they might have"; and to "always protect the safety, interests, and rights of all individuals in the classroom." Parents agree to "always help our child in the best way we know how and we will do whatever it takes for him/her to learn. This also means that we will check our child's homework every night, let him/her call the teacher if there is a problem with the homework, and try to read with him/her every night."

Students promise to "always work, think, and behave in the best way I know how, and I will do whatever it takes for me and my fellow students to learn. This also means that I will complete all my homework every night, I will call my teachers if I have a problem with the homework or a problem with coming to school, and I will raise my hand and ask questions in class if I do not understand something."

KIPP schools are notable for their use of financial rewards to motivate students, which were described at some length in Chapter 3. A profile of the schools in *Time* magazine noted the alignment of the KIPP model with research on the effectiveness of rewards conducted by Harvard's Roland J. Fryer, Jr.

> The Knowledge Is Power Program (KIPP), one of the most successful charter-school networks in the U.S., has been doling out financial incentives for 15 years, using a model that happens to align perfectly with the results of Fryer's study. KIPP students get paid for actions they can control – getting to school on time, participating in class and having a positive attitude – with "money" they can redeem for supplies at the school store. Over the years, KIPP leaders, who now run 82 schools nationwide, have learned a lot about which rewards work and which do not. They have found that speed matters, for example. Recognition, like punishment, works best if it happens quickly. So KIPP schools pay their kids every week.[54]

In 2013, the Mathematica Policy Research group published a multi-year study of KIPP schools and found that after three years in the program the students were 11 months ahead of their public school peers in math, eight months ahead in reading, and 14 months ahead in science.[55] According to KIPP, by the end of eighth grade 62 percent of its students outperform their national peers in math, and 57 percent do so in reading. On state tests, by the end of eighth grade, 94 percent of KIPP classes outperform their local districts in reading; 96 percent do so in math.[56]

KIPP is not the only network of successful charter schools,[57] but KIPP schools illustrate how the charter mechanism can be used to reward students, parents, teachers, and school administrators who set high standards, work together, and use research-proven methods to accelerate learning.

Parent Trigger: California

California Governor Arnold Schwarzenegger signed the nation's first parent trigger law on January 7, 2010.[58] The program grew out of grassroots outrage over the low quality of public schools especially in Los Angeles. As California State Senator Gloria Romero, a Democrat representing Los Angeles and author of the parent trigger bill, told the *Los Angeles Daily News*, "I'm sorry – after a certain point you are no longer credible on the promise that you'll fix it. Parents want change and opportunity now."[59]

Since 2010, some 20 states have considered parent trigger legislation and six (in addition to California) have adopted variations on the plan.[60] The concept is popular: A poll conducted in 2013 found 49 percent of U.S. adults support parent triggers while 40 percent oppose such laws.[61] How do parent triggers work?

In California, participation is limited to parents with children enrolled in a failing public school as defined by the California School Code or in feeder schools (neighborhood primary or middle schools) that send children to a failing school. Schools must be labeled a "program improvement school" for more than three consecutive years for failing to meet federal academic benchmarks, have an Academic Performance Index (the state's benchmark test) of less than 800,[62] and be among the lowest 5 percent of schools in California. The number of schools that can be "triggered" is capped at 75 statewide.

If 50 percent of eligible parents sign a properly designed petition, the local education agency – usually a school district – must implement one of four "school intervention models" specified in the petition. The four models are closure (close the school, fire or reassign the staff, and send the children to better-performing schools nearby), restart (convert the school to an independent charter school), turnaround (replace school leadership and grant new leaders more flexibility), and transformation (turnaround model with added layers of bureaucratic oversight.)

The parent trigger forces school districts to undertake changes that school administrators and staffs otherwise would oppose. The simplicity of the process lowers the cost to parents in terms of the time they must invest in order to improve their children's schools, thereby creating an incentive for them to pay attention to and more actively participate in reform efforts. Teachers and administrators, realizing that parents now wield the power to shut down the school or hand it over to a charter school operator, have new incentives to listen carefully to parents' concerns, focus more on academic success, and join parents in a united quest for excellence.

Closing persistently failing schools and moving children into new schools accelerates student achievement only if better schools are available nearby and can accommodate an influx of students – a problem in large cities with large numbers of failing public schools. Transferring to a new school can be disruptive for the child, parents, and teachers, and the costs must be weighed against the potential benefit for the individual child as well as other children. Most transferring students recover whatever academic ground they lose after one or two years in their new school and then outperform their counterparts who remained behind in the failing school.[63] All students, including those not enrolled in a failing school, benefit when even a small number of schools are closed, because such closures signal to school administrators that failure will not be tolerated.

Allowing parents to petition to have their local public school converted into a charter school is a wise policy choice. Parents often develop loyalty to the personnel of local public schools that can lead them to oppose the opening of a charter school nearby. A parent trigger places the decision in the hands of parents themselves, helping to ensure community support for new charter schools. The conversion option solves problems related to arbitrary caps on the number of charter schools allowed in a city or a state (often negotiated in state capitols as the price of avoiding union opposition) and limited access by charter school operators to surplus school buildings and other resources that public school systems hoard.

California's parent trigger is an innovative and positive piece of public policy, but it is not perfect. Most notably it does not include private school choice – vouchers or scholarships – in the list of options from which parents can choose. This is like giving guests on the ill-fated Titanic a choice of seats on the deck of the sinking ship but forbidding them from using the lifeboats. The "turnaround" and "transformation" models, adopted from the federal Race to the Top legislation, are the weakest of the options available to parents.[64] Merely replacing the existing school management with another version of bureaucratic control offers little assurance that students would benefit.

Another shortcoming of California's law is that it allows local school authorities, who plainly have a conflict of interest, to override the option chosen by parents, potentially undoing many hours of parents' time and crushing raised hopes. Even the risk of such a veto is enough to discourage many parents from going through the considerable effort of circulating a petition. California places severe restrictions on which schools are subject to the law – only the worst 5 percent and no more than 75 schools – and therefore denies use of this powerful tool to millions of parents who might otherwise choose to use it. Why not let parents, rather than state and federal bureaucrats, determine which schools are "failing" and therefore subject to the parent trigger?

Another problem with California's parent trigger law is that it is tied to the federal Race to the Top initiative, which was funded by the 2009 American Recovery and Reinvestment Act. By incorporating by reference federal rules and guidelines, California's legislators have made school reform in their state subject to the past and future judgments of Congress and Washington bureaucrats.

Later in this chapter we will present design guidelines for policymakers and parents who might want a parent trigger law without California's shortcomings. Our reservations aside, the parent trigger is clearly an idea that can move K–12 schools in the right direction by rewarding parents for getting actively involved in school reform efforts and exposing educators and administrators to the risks of closure, competition, and choice.

School Vouchers (Scholarships): Indiana

School vouchers – sometimes called scholarships – expand school choice by giving parents public financial support to choose private schools for their children. In 2012, 29 voucher and tax-credit programs operated in 21 states and the District of Columbia and enrolled 212,000 children.[65] States including Florida, Indiana, Louisiana, and Wisconsin are dramatically expanding their scholarship programs.

In 2011, Indiana adopted the Indiana School Scholarship Program (ISSP), a voucher program for families in Indiana with incomes up to 150 percent of the amount required for the family's children to qualify for the federal free or reduced-price school lunch program.[66] A family of four earning up to $61,000 per year would be eligible to participate in the program. Participation was limited to 7,500 students in the first year and 15,000 in the second, with no cap on enrollment after the second year.

Low-income families qualify for scholarships equal to private school tuition or 90 percent of the state's current share of per-pupil public school spending, whichever is less. Students from households with incomes between that mark and 150 percent of that mark qualify for scholarships equal to tuition or 50 percent of state per-pupil spending, whichever is less. Scholarships for students in grades 1–8 are capped at $4,500, but scholarships for high-school students are not capped.

In 2012–13, more than 9,000 Indiana students received scholarships and nearly 300 schools participated in the ISSP.[67] In 2013 the law was expanded to include children attending failing public schools and special-needs students regardless of family income.[68] The expansion also attached special-education funds of up to $8,350 to the scholarships received by children with special needs such as blindness and learning disabilities.

The law features a fair and non-bureaucratic form of accountability by providing for suspension of scholarship payments for new students if a school fails to rise above either of the lowest two categories of public school performance currently set forth in the school code. Parents are allowed to use their own resources to add to the scholarship if tuition exceeds the value of the voucher, a laudable policy that encourages more parents and schools to participate. ISSP allows schools to retain control over admissions requirements and requires lotteries only if the number of applicants exceeds the number of vacancies.

An especially strong feature of the ISSP is that it erects barriers to increased regulation of participating schools. Fear of excessive regulation is expressed in some quarters as a principal reason to oppose school vouchers.[69] The Indiana law erects at least four barriers to this threat:

- Chapter 4, Section 1(a) memorializes the legislature's intent to preserve the autonomy of private schools by saying "it is the intent of the general assembly to honor the autonomy of nonpublic schools that choose to become eligible schools under this chapter. A nonpublic eligible school is not an agent of the state or federal government." This language is important because it creates a presumption in favor of less rather than more regulation of participating schools and establishes that it is in the public interest to preserve the autonomy of private schools.

- Chapter 4, Section 1(a)(1) says "the department or any other state agency may not in any way regulate the educational program of a nonpublic eligible school that accepts a choice scholarship under this chapter, including the regulation of curriculum content, religious instruction or activities, classroom teaching, teacher and staff hiring requirements, and other activities carried out by the eligible school."

- Chapter 4, Section 1(a)(2) states: "the creation of the choice scholarship program does not expand the regulatory authority of the state, the state's officers, or a school corporation to impose additional regulation of nonpublic schools beyond those necessary to enforce the requirements of the school scholarship program in place on July 1, 2011."

- Chapter 4, Section 3(a) reads: "An eligible school may not discriminate on the basis of race, color, or national origin." This language properly forbids discrimination on the basis of race, color, or national origin but not religion or other factors that may be important to a school's culture. This matter is settled law. So long as a voucher program empowers parents to choose public or private schools, and does not tilt incentives toward religious schools or toward schools teaching or practicing a particular faith, a religious element in admissions and classroom teaching is acceptable.

The ISSP isn't perfect legislation. The cap on the value of scholarships for grades K–8 is too low and not indexed for inflation or state per-pupil spending. Nationally, secular private schools charge an average of $15,945 a year in tuition, more than three times the value of the scholarship provided by the ISSP. The cap of only $4,500 for scholarships for grades K–8 will pose a barrier to entry for some private schools. This "bad" provision is partially offset by the facts that there is no similar cap on the value of high-school scholarships and parents are allowed to supplement the scholarships with their own tuition payments.

By limiting participation to low-income families, the ISSP requires parents to share their tax returns and other personal information with schools and government agencies to determine their eligibility for grants of different sizes, an invasion of privacy that will reduce participation. Such means-testing also creates disincentives for parents to accept new jobs or report additional income if they believe doing so will disqualify them from future tuition scholarships. The loss of a scholarship as income rises is similar to a high marginal tax on earnings, which extensive research shows leads to less effort and fewer hours of work.[70]

The ISSP limits participation to accredited schools, which Indiana currently over-regulates. It also requires participating schools to administer the state's achievement tests rather than giving participating schools their choice of norm-referenced tests. A better choice would be to require schools to administer and release the results of norm-referenced tests of their choice. There are several accepted national norm-referenced tests available that would produce results at least as meaningful as the state's tests.

Finally, the ISSP tries to micro-manage the teaching of civics and American history, perhaps to head off criticism that participating schools might teach anti-American doctrines. Concern about the possible misuse of public funds to support schools that teach violence or hatred of America is legitimate, but it is addressed simply and correctly for all schools in Chapter 4, Section 1(g): "An eligible school, charter school, or public school shall not teach the violent overthrow of the government of the United States." The ISSP goes far beyond this, presenting some two-and-a-half pages of detailed instructions on what participating schools must teach.

Despite its flaws, the Indiana School Scholarship Program serves as a good model for legislators considering drafting legislation for voucher programs in their states. As the program expands it could benefit millions of children in Indiana and prompt other states to follow Indiana's lead.

Education Savings Accounts: Arizona

As vouchers and tax credits move more substantially from theory to practice in cities and states across the country, greater attention is being focused on matters of program design. One design feature that could boost the effectiveness of school choice and help minimize the threat of increased regulation of participating schools is education savings accounts, or ESAs.[71]

ESAs are tax-sheltered savings accounts similar to individual retirement accounts (IRAs) and the newer health savings accounts (HSAs). In the case of IRAs and HSAs, employers and individuals make deposits into the accounts and spending is limited or not allowed until the individual reaches a certain age for IRAs, and only for health care expenses for HSAs. An ESA operates similarly but with spending limited to education expenses and with governments depositing into the ESA each year the money collected from taxes that would otherwise go to public schools. Parents can then draw on the account to pay for tuition at the public or private schools of their choice, or pay for tutoring and other educational expenses for their child. At the end of a student's K–12 career, anything left in the account could be applied to college tuition or technical training. When the student reaches a certain age (19, 21, or 23 are often suggested), anything left in the account would revert to taxpayers.

ESAs are not a new idea.[72] They were the central feature of a proposal made in 1992 by The Heartland Institute to the New American Schools Development Corporation as part of a national competition for "breakthrough" ideas for school reform. The proposal placed in the top 4 percent of 686 competitors but did not receive funding. A year later, ESAs were part of the first modern school choice initiative to appear on a ballot – the 1993 California Parental Choice in Education Initiative. Three years later, the California Educational Freedom Amendment contained similar language. Both initiatives were defeated. ESAs have been proposed by several researchers, including the authors, in the years since then.[73]

In 2011, Arizona became the first state to adopt education savings accounts into law.[74] Called "Empowerment Scholarship Accounts," originally only children with special needs who were previously enrolled in public schools were eligible. Children in failing schools, children in military families, and adopted and foster children became eligible in 2013.[75] Grants originally were set at 90 percent of what the school would have received from the state minus another 3 percent for administration costs, approximately $3,000. In 2013 the amount was changed to 90 percent of state per-pupil charter school funding, approximately $6,000, plus whatever additional funds are allocated for special-needs children.[76]

Parents who are allowed to set up accounts agree to enroll their child in private or online schools or to homeschool their children. Instruction must cover reading, grammar, mathematics, social studies, and science. Participating students are not required to take tests. Arizona State Sen. Rick Murphy, a sponsor of the 2013 legislation that expanded the program, said "I agreed to include the so-called accountability provisions with the exception of a testing requirement. I don't think a testing requirement is necessary because parents are the accountability. You either trust them to make good choices for their child or you don't."[77] He added, "The majority of private schools already provide a nationally norm-referenced test. In the rare schools that don't, it's probably because the parents don't see it as valuable and haven't demanded it, and it shouldn't be forced on them."

Annual ESA deposits made to date have ranged from $1,500 to

$27,500.[78] Parents use debit cards to pay expenses and send receipts to the Department of Education each quarter for approval. Allowable uses for funds are listed in the table on the following page.

The program enrolled only 75 children in its first year and 400 in its second, but with the new eligibility rules and larger scholarship amount adopted in 2012, its supporters expect enrollment to grow rapidly.[79] No doubt the program could be improved: universal eligibility would dramatically boost participation. But otherwise the program has the admirable features of minimal rules, regulations, and bureaucracy. The program also has withstood the usual legal challenges from teachers unions and other entities opposed to change.

Arizona's Empowerment Scholarship Accounts demonstrate how ESAs are a promising way to bring competition and choice into K–12 education. Supporters of ESAs recognize that learning increasingly takes place outside brick-and-mortar buildings and learning environments can be designed to accommodate the needs of individual students, meaning tuition may not be the only or even the largest expense confronting a highly engaged parent. Allowing parents to keep money left in the accounts at the end of each year gives parents a financial incentive to find efficient ways to accelerate learning and for providers to compete on the basis of price rather than only promises of high quality.

ESAs could make school choice more popular among suburban parents who tend to think their government schools are high quality but impose too great a tax burden. Per-student spending for suburban high schools often exceeds $16,000, more than even relatively expensive private schools typically charge for tuition. With a universal ESA program in place, some of those parents would be tempted to enroll their children in a private school charging, say, $12,000 a year in tuition and to place the remaining $4,000 in the student's ESA.

ESAs, finally, could protect parents and schools from increased government regulation, which is always a threat under charter school and scholarship programs. An ESA would stand between governments and schools, with tax dollars first deposited into the student's account and then tuition or fees paid by check or debit card by the parent or guardian. Schools would not receive payment directly from government agencies.

Allowable Uses of Funds from
Empowerment Scholarship Accounts

- Tuition, fees, and/or required textbooks at a qualified school. A qualified school is defined as a private school in Arizona serving kindergarten, grades one through 12 or a preschool for disabled students. The school must not discriminate on the basis of race, color, or national origin.

- Educational therapies and/or services for the student from a licensed or accredited practitioner or provider.

- Tutoring services from an individual or provider who is accredited by a state, regional, or national accrediting organization.

- Purchase of curriculum, generally defined as a complete course of study for a particular content area or grade level.

- Tuition and/or fees for a private online learning program.

- Fees for nationally standardized norm-referenced achievement tests, Advanced Placement exams, and/or other exams related to college or university admissions such as ACT or SAT.

- Contributions to a qualified college savings plan, as authorized by 11 United States Code §529, for the benefit of the student.

- Tuition, fees, and/or required textbooks at a public community college or university in Arizona.

- Account fees charged by a bank administering the ESA.

Source: Aiden Fleming, "Empowerment Scholarship Accounts Information Session," Arizona Department of Education, September 27, 2011, [PowerPoint] http://www.azed.gov/esa/faq/. See source for original phrasing of these provisions.

Best Practices

Four types of school choice programs are described above: charter schools, parent triggers, school vouchers (or scholarships), and education savings accounts. The successful or promising examples presented offer guidance to policymakers and parents who want to expand school choice in their own cities and states. Some of the best practices for each follow.

Charter Schools

Charter schools have been around for some 20 years, and states vary in policies concerning their funding and accountability. A large body of research exists on best practices.[80] Some of the more important insights include:

- Do not limit or arbitrarily cap the number of charter schools or the number of students who can attend charter schools.

- Do not attempt to overly specify what charter schools must look like by, for example, specifying student-teacher ratios, seat time, curriculum, or facilities, or what types of groups may be allowed to start charter schools.

- Exempt charter schools from most school district laws and regulations, retaining only laws most necessary to safety, civil rights, financial stability, and accountability to parents. Follow North Carolina's lead and exempt charter schools from teacher certification requirements.[81]

- Fund charter schools at a level close to the amount the public schools receive in order to ensure real competition and choice. Although the amount need not be 100 percent, since there is waste in traditional public schools that ought to be squeezed out by competition, 50 percent is probably too little to attract entrepreneurs and support high-quality schools.

- Establish alternative authorizers. Allowing only a local school district to authorize a charter school often leads to too few schools to meet the demand. Statewide authorizers independent of the local public school district are necessary to overcome the conflicts of interest and lack of expertise on charter schools that plague many local school districts.

■ Establish clarity and consensus about what school outcomes must be maintained for schools to retain their charters. Set clear rules regarding independent audits of school finances and performance and how results are to be reported to parents and public authorities.

■ Close charter schools that are failing to meet minimum performance thresholds. In return for flexibility, charter schools accept responsibility for failure. The closing of some charter schools should be viewed as evidence the system is working, not that it is broken.

Parent Triggers

California's parent trigger was a product of the state's political and economic environment. Other states face similar pressures and choices, but they do not have to make the same choices California's lawmakers made. Some design guidelines include:[82]

■ The parents of children attending *all* public schools should be able to petition to reform their schools. There should be no arbitrary cap on the number of students or schools that could participate.

■ School boards should not be given the authority to overrule a petition by parents, or a process for appealing such a decision should be made explicit in the trigger law. Public funding for litigation and representation of parents during the appeals process should be provided by the state.

■ The flawed turnaround and transformation models should be replaced with vouchers or scholarships to pay tuition at participating public or private schools.

■ Boards or committees created to oversee the process should have supermajority representation by parents since teachers and school board members have manifest conflicts of interest. Candidates for such boards should be ruled ineligible if they work for a school district or have a spouse who works for one.

■ The petition process should be carefully spelled out in the legislation to prevent opponents of reform from using litigation and pettifoggery to block the clear intent of parents.

■ Resources should be made available to parents so they can make informed choices about whether to begin a petition drive, how to word the petition, how to gather signatures, how to submit the petition, and so on. This could take the form of modest grants given competitively to nonprofit civic organizations.

■ Although the federal Race to the Top program provided an impetus for enacting the parent trigger in California, it is not necessary or desirable that other states tie their trigger legislation so closely to the federal program.

Vouchers (Scholarships)

Voucher or scholarship programs have been designed to achieve a variety of goals such as benefiting special-needs children, rescuing children in inner cities from low-performing public schools, and saving taxpayers money. The focus in this chapter has been to use scholarships to transform public education, which means changing the way K–12 schooling is provided for all children. With that goal in mind, here are important best practices.[83]

■ Allow all parents to choose. This may require phasing in the program over several years, perhaps by grade level or starting with poor families and then moving to universal eligibility. Parents are reluctant to move their children from their current schools, and even private institutions that must compete to survive require some time to adapt to new rules.

■ Allow all schools to compete. Don't limit participation to only nonprofit, secular, or even accredited schools. Regulate primarily for safety and transparency and not for policies unrelated to student achievement such as class size or seat time.

■ Set the value of a scholarship at between half and three-quarters of current public per-pupil spending and allow schools to charge more than that amount, with parents making up the difference. This ensures that the scholarships are sufficiently generous to prompt the creation of new schools while also making it possible to provide scholarships to children who already attend private schools without increasing total spending.

■ Fund the scholarships out of current per-pupil allocations from state and local tax sources. This can help avoid protracted political and legal battles by leaving in place current (often complex) funding formulas that have evolved over years of negotiations and political compromises.

■ No new regulations should be imposed on schools that choose to participate in the scholarship program. Indiana's School Scholarship Program offers a good model in this regard.

■ If the scholarship program requires that students be tested, then schools and parents should be allowed to choose among different norm-referenced tests rather than be required to take a single state-administered test.

■ Place administration of the program in the hands of a neutral oversight authority independent of the public school establishment, including the state school board. Consider the state treasurer or comptroller since they presumably are less likely to have conflicts of interest.

Education Savings Accounts

Education savings accounts (ESAs) have been tried in only one state, Arizona, and that program is too new and too small to produce many lessons for reformers. Many of the best practices set forth above for scholarship programs, however, apply equally to ESAs. They need not be repeated here.

Misuse of funds is likely to be a bigger problem with ESAs than with scholarship programs because a much larger universe of vendors will be qualified to receive payments from the accounts. Asking vendors to pre-register with the state could reduce fraud but also greatly reduce parental choices. Either way, the state will require sophisticated data processing and auditing systems built around debit cards, a competence that private-sector companies have but the government in a given state may not.

ESAs require more from parents than traditional public schools or even scholarship programs. Parents must be educators, accountants, program coordinators, liaisons to the Department of Education and other agencies, and administrators.[84] Some parents will be overwhelmed and seek to re-enroll their children in local public schools, which may be aggressively downsizing and not able to accommodate the returning students. Many parents will turn to the state for guidance. The state, in partnership with public and private schools and the emerging digital learning industry, must be prepared to field a team of advisors or coaches to lend their assistance.

As parents use ESAs to take their children's education further and further away from the traditional K–12 school model, difficult issues of grade advancement, graduation, and remediation will need to be addressed. Should a 10-year-old child who is performing at a ninth-grade level in math but a third-grade level in English be advanced from the fifth to the sixth grade? Should advancement, graduation, and a high-school diploma be determined solely by passing exams? Will colleges and employers accept such diplomas? Moving from seat-time requirements toward demonstrated mastery of knowledge and skills, sometimes called competency education, raises public policy issues that need to be addressed.[85] ESAs require these issues be addressed, perhaps sooner than the political process can provide answers.

Conclusion

Schooling in the U.S. is genuinely in a state of crisis. It is unrewarding to students, parents, educators, and the nation as a whole. It continues to threaten society and the economy. "Reform" has been tried and found wanting. Transformation is required. School choice can transform K–12 education not in some distant future but right now in states whose leaders have the courage to adopt the necessary policies.

School choice means giving schools the flexibility they need to thrive while simultaneously giving parents the freedom to choose among schools competing to serve their children. This process of competition and choice is so commonplace in the rest of our lives that we hardly notice it, yet it is conspicuously absent in most of public K–12 education today. To improve education substantially, we need to revisit the nineteenth century decision to place government in control of most of the nation's schools. We need to expand parents' choice over their children's schooling.

Charter schools show the power of competition and choice in education. Their rapid spread across the country shows they enjoy bipartisan support and the best research finds they produce superior academic results. KIPP schools, in particular, are proving that flexibility and choice can motivate students, parents, teachers, and administrators to work together to achieve excellence.

After more than 20 years, charter schools still enroll only 3 percent of all students. Opposition to their establishment is often intense outside big cities, and even in big cities there are efforts to roll back the gains made by charter schools by re-regulating them. Parent triggers – laws that allow parents to petition to have their local public schools shut down or be converted into charter schools, or receive scholarships to send their children to private schools of their choice – are a step further than where charters can take us. Why not empower a majority of parents to vote to transform their local schools?

More radical than the parent trigger are vouchers or scholarships. Why should a majority of parents have to vote before even one parent is allowed to use the public dollars already committed to his or her child's education to pay tuition at a better, private school? Greater parental choice is necessary to get past the 3 percent or 4 percent participation wall that charter schools are facing. The fact that 21 states and the District of Columbia now have voucher or tax-credit programs suggests these advanced forms of school choice are catching on around the country. Indiana shows what a promising statewide program looks like.

Even more disruptive of the status quo than vouchers are education savings accounts. Why should parents be allowed to use the public dollars raised for their child's education only on private-school tuition when digital learning technologies are making traditional brick-and-mortar schools obsolete? Why not allow them to assemble a portfolio of schools, teachers, online courses, and testing services that is uniquely tailored for their child? Who better than parents to assemble such a plan, possibly with advice from experts and experienced friends? Arizona is conducting what may be the most exciting school choice experiment taking place in America today.

Schools of choice are highly effective because they benefit from the altered behavior of all parties involved. Students are more motivated when they attend schools they helped choose or their parents chose for them. Administrators and teachers of schools that parents choose are rewarded with increased enrollment and revenue. Parents who take the time to choose a high-quality school for their children and who express their concerns to teachers and school administrators are rewarded when the schools are responsive to their concerns and requests. Even taxpayers are rewarded since schools of choice generally spend less than traditional public schools.

Notes

1. Margaret Diane LeCompte and Anthony Gary Dworkin, *Giving Up on School: Student Dropouts and Teacher Burnouts* (Newbury Park, CA: Corwin Press, Inc., 1991), p. 228.

2. National Commission on Excellence in Education, *A Nation at Risk* (Washington, DC: U.S. Department of Education, 1983).

3. *Ibid.*

4. Bruce K. Maclaury, foreword to John E. Chubb and Terry M. Moe, *Politics, Markets, and America's Schools* (Washington, DC: The Brookings Institution, 1990), p. ix.

5. Margaret Diane LeCompte and Anthony Gary Dworkin, *supra* note 1, p. 231.

6. *Ibid.*

7. Paul E. Peterson, ed., *Our Schools and Our Future ... Are We Still at Risk?* (Stanford, CA: Hoover Press, 2003).

8. Jim Waters, "Still Mediocre Results on 2011 Nation's Report Card," *School Reform News*, November 2011.

9. National Assessment of Educational Progress, *The Nation's Report Card: Science 2011*, May 2012, National Center for Education Statistics, U.S. Department of Education, https://nces.ed.gov/nationsreportcard/pubs/main2011/2012465.asp, viewed on July 5, 2013.

10. Jim Waters, *supra* note 8.

11. Program for International Student Assessment (PISA), U.S. Department of Education, National Center for Education Statistics, *Digest of Education Statistics, 2011* (NCES 2012-001), Chapter 6.

12. Lyndsey Layton, "High School Graduation Rate Rises in U.S.," *Washington Post*, March 19, 2012, citing a report from America's Promise.

13. *Ibid.*

14. Dan Lips, Shanea Watkins, Ph.D., and John Fleming, "Does Spending More on Education Improve Academic Achievement?" *Backgrounder*, The Heritage Foundation, September 8, 2008, citing Department of Education figures.

15. Andrew LeFevre, *Report Card on American Education: A State-by-State Analysis*, (Washington, DC: American Legislative Exchange Council, 2006).

16. Caroline M. Hoxby, "School Choice and School Productivity, or Could School Choice Be a Tide that Lifts All Boats?" in Caroline Hoxby, ed., *Economics of School Choice* (Chicago, IL: University of Chicago Press, 2001). Also by the same author, "Productivity in Education: The Quintessential Upstream Industry," *Southern Economic Journal* 71, no. 2 (October 2004): 208–31.

17. Caroline M. Hoxby, "School Choice and School Productivity," *ibid.*

18. Organization for Economic Cooperation and Development (OECD), *Education at a Glance 2007.*

19. National Center for Education Statistics, *Digest of Education Statistics, 2007*, Table 80.

20. *Ibid.*, Table 61.

21. Robert B. Everhart, ed., *The Public School Monopoly* (San Francisco, CA: Pacific Research Institute, 1982).

22. Charles L. Glenn, *Choice of Schools in Six Nations* (Washington, DC: U.S. Department of Education, December 1989); by the same author, *Educational Freedom in Eastern Europe* (Washington, DC: Cato Institute, 1995).

23. Christopher T. Cross, foreword to Charles L. Glenn, *Choice of Schools in Six Nations*, *ibid.*, p. ix.

24. Friedman Foundation for Educational Choice, "Mothers Show Strong Support for School Choice in National Survey," May 8, 2013, news release, http://www.edchoice.org/Newsroom/News/Mothers-Show-Strong-Support-for-School-Choice-in-National-Survey.aspx.

25. Terry M. Moe, *Schools, Vouchers, and the American Public* (Washington, DC: Brookings Institution, 2001).

26. Sam Redding, *Parents and Learning* (Geneva, Switzerland: International Bureau of Education, 2000), www.illinoisparents.org/pr/English/Booklets/Parents%20and%20Learning.pdf.

27. Eric A. Hanushek, *et al.*, *Making Schools Work* (Washington, DC: Brookings Institution, 1994); Frederick M. Hess, *Common Sense School Reform* (New York, NY: Palgrave Macmillan, 2004).

28. Edwin Locke and Gary P. Latham, "Building a Practically Useful Theory of Goal Setting and Task Motivation," *American Psychologist* 57, no. 9 (September 2002): 705–17; William H. Schmidt, Richard Houang, and Sharif Shakrani, *International Lessons about National Standards* (Washington, DC: Thomas B. Fordham Foundation, August 2009).

29. Roland Fryer Jr., "Injecting Successful Charter School Strategies into Traditional Public Schools," *Working Paper*, National Bureau of Economic Research, January 2012, http://www.economics.harvard.edu/ faculty/fryer/files/charter-school-strategies.pdf.

30. *Ibid.*

31. See the works by John Chubb and Terry Moe and James Q. Wilson cited in Chapter 2.

32. Donald T. Campbell, "Assessing the Impact of Planned Social Change," *Evaluation and Program Planning* 2 (1979): 85.

33. Margaret Diane LeCompte and Anthony Gary Dworkin, *supra* note 1, pp. 218, 226.

34. Melissa Roderick, John Q. Easton, and Penny Bender Sebring, *The Consortium on Chicago School Research: A New Model for the Role of Research in Supporting Urban School Reform* (Chicago, IL: The Consortium on Chicago School Research at the University of Chicago Urban Education Institute, 2009), p. 22.

35. *Ibid.*, citing William Easterly, *The White Man's Burden: Why the West's Efforts to Aid the Rest Have Done So Much Ill and So Little Good* (New York, NY: Penguin Press, 2006).

36. Amitai Etzioni, foreword in Clifford W. Cobb, *Responsive Schools, Renewed Communities* (San Francisco, CA: ICS Press, 1992), p. xi.

37. John E. Coons and Stephen D. Sugarman, *Education by Choice: The Case for Family Control* (1978, reprint, Troy, NY: Educator's International Press, Inc., 1999).

38. Herbert J. Walberg and Joseph L. Bast, "Can Parents Choose the Best Schools for their Children?" *Economics of Education Review* 23 (2004): 431–40.

39. *Ibid.*

40. John Merrifield, *The School Choice Wars* (Lanham, MD: Scarecrow Press Inc., 2001), p. 77.

41. William G. Howell, Martin R. West, and Paul E. Peterson, "What Americans Think About Their Schools," *Education Next* 7, no. 4 (Fall 2007): 12–26.

42. Center for Education Reform, "Charter School Law," http://www.edreform.com/issues/choice-charter-schools/laws-legislation/, viewed on July 9, 2013. The eight states that do not allow charter schools are Alabama, Kentucky, Montana, Nebraska, North Dakota, South Dakota, Vermont, and West Virginia.

43. *Ibid.*

44. For example, see Devora H. Davis and Margaret E. Raymond, "Choices for Studying Choice: Assessing Charter School Effectiveness Using Two Quasi-experimental Methods," *Economics of Education Review* 31, no. 2 (April 2012).

45. Caroline M. Hoxby, "Achievement in Charter Schools and Regular Public Schools in the United States: Understanding the Differences," December 2004, http://post.economics.harvard.edu/faculty/hoxby/papers.html.

46. Bryan C. Hassel, *Charter School Achievement: What We Know* (Chapel Hill, NC: Public Impact, July 2005).

47. Caroline M. Hoxby and Jonah E. Rockoff, "The Impact of Charter Schools on Student Achievement," November 2004, http://post.economics.harvard.edu/faculty/hoxby/papers.html.

48. See Herbert J. Walberg, *School Choice: The Findings* (Washington, DC: Cato Institute, 2007), Chapter 3 for a detailed survey of the literature.

49. Michelle Croft, Susan Dynarski, Caroline Hoxby, Tom Loveless, Mark Schneider, Grover Whitehurst, and John Witte, *Charter Schools: A Report on Rethinking the Federal Role in Education* (Washington, DC: Brookings Institution, December 2010),

http://www.brookings.edu/~/media/research/files/reports/2010/12/16%20charter%20scho
ols/1216_charter_schools.pdf.

50. Accenture, "Accenture Awards KIPP – Knowledge Is Power Program – an
Additional US $3.3 Million to Equip Young People with Career Readiness Skills,"
undated news release, http://careers.accenture.com/us-en/about/news/Pages/
acn-awards-kipp-knowledge-power-program.aspx.

51. KIPP Foundation, "Five Pillars," http://www.kipp.org/FAB8BFD0-B631-
11E1-A076005056883C4D, viewed July 8, 2013.

52. John E. Chubb and Terry M. Moe, *Politics, Markets and America's Schools*
(Washington, DC: Brookings Institution, 1990).

53. KIPP Foundation, "KIPP Commitment to Excellence," http://www.kipp.org/files/
dmfile/KIPP_Commitment_to_Excellence_Sample.pdf, viewed July 8, 2013.

54. Amanda Ripley, "Should Kids Be Bribed to Do Well in School?" *Time*, April 8,
2010, http://www.time.com/time/magazine/article/0,9171,1978758,00.html.

55. Christian Clark Tuttle, *et al.*, *KIPP Middle Schools: Impacts on Achievement and
Other Outcomes* (Washington, DC: Mathematica Policy Group, February 27 2013),
http://www.mathematica-mpr.com/publications/pdfs/education/KIPP_middle.pdf.

56. KIPP, "Are KIPP Students Progressing and Achieving Academically?"
http://www.kipp.org/question3.

57. Others include Aspire, BASIS Schools, GreenDot, National Heritage Academies, and
Rocketship (described in Chapter 10). See Sean Cavanagh, "Prominent Charter Networks
Eye Fresh Territory," *Education Week*, July 5, 2012.

58. The following discussion is based on Joseph L. Bast, Bruno Behrend, Ben Boychuk,
and Marc Oestreich, "The Parent Trigger: A Model for Transforming Education," *Policy
Brief*, The Heartland Institute, August 2010. See also Ben Boychuk, "The 'Parent
Trigger' in California: Some Lessons from the Experience So Far," *Policy Brief*, The
Heartland Institute, October 2011.

59. Connie Llanos, "Parents Pulling 'Trigger' on School," *Los Angeles Daily News*,
February 14, 2010.

60. The National Conference of State Legislatures maintains a website at
http://www.ncsl.org/research/education/state-parent-trigger-laws.aspx that tracks parent
trigger legislation around the country.

61. Paul DiPerna, "Schooling in America Survey: What Do Mothers Say About K–12
Education?" *Polling Paper No. 15*, Friedman Foundation for Educational Choice, May 8,
2013, pp. 22–3.

62. Academic Performance Index (API) scores in California are a compilation of a
school's state standardized test scores, on a scale of 200 to 1,000. The California
Department of Education expects all schools eventually to attain APIs of at least 800.

63. Caroline M. Hoxby and Jonah E. Rockoff, "Findings from the City of Big
Shoulders," *Education Next*, Fall 2005.

64. See the description of these two reform options in Chapter 4.

65. Andrew Campanella, Malcom Glenn, and Lauren Perry, *Hope for America's Children: School Choice Year Book 2010–11*, Alliance for School Choice, 2011.

66. Joseph L. Bast, "The Indiana School Scholarship Act (House Bill 1003): Commentary and Analysis," *Policy Brief*, The Heartland Institute, June 2011.

67. Rachel Sheffield, "Indiana Expands Voucher Program," *School Reform News*, May 2013, http://news.heartland.org/newspaper_article/2013/05/07/ indiana_expand_voucher_program.

68. *Ibid.*

69. See the sources cited in Joseph L. Bast, "Why Conservatives and Libertarians Should Support Vouchers," *Independent Review* 7, no. 2 (Fall–Winter 2002): 265–76.

70. Alan Reynolds, "Marginal Tax Rates," in David R. Henderson, ed., *Concise Encyclopedia of Economics* (Indianapolis, IN: Liberty Fund, Inc., 2005).

71. This section is based on Joseph L. Bast, "Time to Consider Education Savings Accounts," *School Reform News*, September 2005, http://www.schoolreform-news.org/article/17659.

72. Joseph L. Bast, "A Short History of Education Savings Accounts," *Policy Brief*, The Heartland Institute, June 13, 2005, http://heartland.org/sites/all/modules/custom/heartland_migration/files/pdfs/17458.pdf.

73. *Ibid.* See also John Charles, *Cascade Update*, Summer 2005; Pearl Rock Kane, "Choice & Freedom, Milton Friedman on Education," *Education Next*, Winter 2003, http://educationnext.org/choicefreedom/; Herbert Walberg and Joseph L. Bast, *Education and Capitalism* (Stanford, CA: Hoover Institution, 2003); Joseph L. Bast, "The Heartland Plan for Illinois: Model School Voucher Legislation," *Policy Study #98*, The Heartland Institute, May 2002; Joseph L. Bast, Herbert Walberg, and Robert Genetski, "The Heartland Report on School Finance for Illinois," *Policy Study*, The Heartland Institute, May 1996.

74. Louisiana and Utah have small programs called "course choice" that give parents and guardians public funds to pay for individual courses delivered by private providers, which is similar to the education savings account idea. For more about how those programs work, see Danielle Dreilinger, "State's Course Choice Program to Give Students Option to Take Outside Classes, But Financing and Implementation Still Face Hurdles," January 12, 2013, and "Louisiana's Course Choice Pilot Program Now Full," February 20, 2013, both at Everything New Orleans, www.nola.com.

75. Arizona Department of Education, "Empowerment Scholarship," http://www.azed.gov/esa/.

76. Ashley Bateman, "Arizona Expands K–12 Education Accounts," *School Reform News*, June 28, 2013.

77. *Ibid.*

78. Aiden Fleming, "Empowerment Scholarship Accounts Informational Slideshow," Arizona Department of Education, September 27, 2011, http://www.azed.gov/esa/faq/.

79. Jonathan Butcher, "Arizona's Education Savings Accounts Turn Two," *School Reform News*, October 20, 2012, http://news.heartland.org/newspaper-article/2012/10/20/arizonas-education-savings-accounts-turn-two.

80. National Association of Charter School Authorizers, *Principles & Standards for Quality Charter School Authorizing*, 2012, http://www.qualitycharters.org/policy/principles-and-standards; U.S. Department of Education, "Nonregulatory Guidance, Title V, Part D, Charter School Program," July 2004, www.ed.gov/policy/elsec/guid/cspguidance03.doc; Center for Education Reform, "Charter School Law," http://www.edreform.com/issues/choice-charter-schools/laws-legislation/.

81. Jane S. Shaw and Zachary Williams, "A License to Innovate?" The John William Pope Center for Higher Education Policy, July 4, 2013, http://www.popecenter.org/commentaries/article.html?id=2869.

82. Joseph L. Bast and Joy Pullmann, "The Parent Trigger: Justification and Design Guidelines," *Policy Brief*, The Heartland Institute, November 2012, http://heartland.org/policy-documents/parent-trigger-justification-and-design-guidelines.

83. For more detail see Chapter 12 of Herbert J. Walberg and Joseph L. Bast, *Education and Capitalism*, *supra* note 73, pp. 289–315.

84. Aiden Fleming, *supra* note 78.

85. Susan Patrick and Chris Sturgis, *Necessary for Success: Building Mastery of World-Class Skills, A State Policymakers Guide to Competency Education* (CompetencyWorks and the International Association for K–12 Online Learning (iNACOL), 2013), http://www.competencyworks.org/wp-content/uploads/2013/02/inacol_cw_issuebrief_building_mastery_final.pdf.

Conclusion

Over the course of some 180 pages and 300 endnotes, we have gone from a theoretical analysis of the effects of rewards on motivation to descriptions of school choice programs in places such as Arizona and Indiana that are transforming K–12 education in the United States. Along the way we have challenged many traditionally accepted ideas about how schools work. In their place we have described research in behavioral psychology and economics that leads to best practices. Let us briefly retrace the steps.

Popular writers claim to have found evidence that rewards in education – as Alfie Kohn put it, everything from praise, A's, and gold stars to incentive plans – do not work because they "extinguish internal motivation." Upon closer inspection, the research these writers cite is selective, based mostly on small and flawed studies largely focused on the short-term behavior of college students and not on the life-long habits and skills that matter in real life. Rigorous research shows that properly designed rewards achieve desired changes in behavior. That research also suggests not rewarding learning and other good behavior can handicap students for the rest of their lives – a stark contrast to the assertions of Kohn and his compatriots.

Similarly, we found popular authors claiming mainstream economics doesn't demonstrate the importance of incentives in everyday life. Economists, they say, assume we all act perfectly rationally all the time, an assumption easily shown to be false. Their claims fail upon close inspection. The quality of the research cited by such critics is vastly inferior to that used by mainstream economists to explain a wide range of choices made every day. Economists do not need to assume perfect rationality to demonstrate how incentives affect learning and other behavior.

We then described the research on the use of rewards to motivate students to learn. This research demonstrated the effectiveness of rewards convincingly and repeatedly. Young children often can be strongly influenced by praise and other recognition. Successful programs also include paying students for studying, turning in homework on time, taking optional exams, enrolling in Advanced Placement courses, reading books, and coming to class on time. An appropriate theory of incentives explains why rewards that are appropriate for young children may not be appropriate for older students, why rewards that are long delayed tend to be less effective, and how reward systems that don't align with or respect a student's own interests, knowledge, and needs are unlikely to work.

Incentives also operate at the level of institutions. The literature is replete with examples of goods and services delivered in a competitive marketplace that cost less and are of higher quality than those delivered by government monopolies. The absence of rewards in public K–12 schools has led schools to operate, in the words of John Chubb and Terry Moe, "like bureaucratic agencies" rather than teams that come together to achieve a shared vision. When schools are required to compete for students and tuition, academic achievement, efficiency, and attractiveness to parents tend to improve substantially.

Greater use of incentives in education faces a potential problem: Effective incentive systems require SMART goals (Specific, Measurable, Attainable, Realistic, and Time-bound), but who should set the goals for K–12 education in the U.S.? America's political heritage and the contemporary popular embrace of cultural diversity mean a one-size-fits-all national education system similar to those in Europe and elsewhere is simply not an attractive option. In Chapter 11 we showed how school choice solves this problem by allowing schools to respond to the preferences of parents and guardians.

The second part of the book examined how parents and teachers can use rewards to assist children's learning at home, in elementary schools, and in high schools. For the very young, frequent rewards are a natural and appropriate part of parenting and an effective way to teach the important life skills of self-discipline, deferred gratification, and perseverance or "grit." Several kinds of rewards are effective in elementary schools including verbal praise, rewards built into lessons, small tokens (stickers, parties, and prizes), grades, arts incentives, money (real or play), and student-initiated rewards. Contrary to the views of many "progressive" educators, these incentives and rewards are popular with parents, teachers, and students precisely because they work so well.

As children get older, incentives help them focus on and practice doing things that aren't necessarily easy or entertaining. By high school, students face serious distractions from learning and may be acting out against authority figures around them, not a productive or beneficial response to the challenges they face. Combating these tendencies requires parents, teachers, and others in the community working together to provide rewards for taking small or interim steps today that will lead to the establishment of longer-term objectives too far into the future to motivate most children, such as admission to a good college or a career in a valued occupation.

In middle school and high school, appropriately designed reward systems require presenting lessons as opportunities for discovery and mastery rather than just following instructions, showing how acquiring new information and skills will increase students' "wealth" (their material belongings as well as their store of knowledge and skills), and making special efforts to show how grades or disciplinary actions are appropriate and fair. These practices take students' interests seriously and create rewards that are aligned with them. "Self-teaching," particularly through online technology, reduces the student cost of learning and consequently elevates the reward received by students who make the effort to plan their studying, monitor their progress, and seek out sources of information on their own.

The final part of the book recommended public policies that accelerate learning by being consistent with the theory and practice of rewards in education. The first policy recommendation is to make greater use of tests with rewards. We refuted a litany of objections to tests, many of them based on past experiences with poorly designed tests, and summarized some of the extensive research (expertly reviewed by Richard Phelps) showing how setting goals and measuring progress increases student motivation and performance, how frequent testing results in greater learning, and how giving students detailed analyses of their test results helps them identify their weaknesses and increases their learning.

Our second policy recommendation is performance-based pay for teachers. Teacher effectiveness varies considerably and those differences have major effects on student achievement. Good teachers are not presently rewarded for their successes or additional efforts, and ineffective teachers often receive pay increases and pension benefits based solely on years of experience. Performance-based pay would attract people with higher skills to the teaching profession and keep the most skillful from leaving. Available research suggests this would lead to a considerable rise in student achievement.

Our third policy recommendation is to expand the use of digital learning – the combination of online adaptive testing and instruction made possible by new technologies, software, and the Internet. Digital learning is making rewards for learning more appropriate, timely, and attuned to the interests and abilities of students, thereby opening the door to a major expansion of their effective use.

Our fourth and final policy recommendation is to give schools the flexibility they need to thrive while simultaneously giving parents the freedom to choose among schools competing to serve their children. School choice, almost uniquely among the reform opportunities considered by policymakers today, has the power to truly transform K–12 education. Charter schools, already operating in 42 states, are the most common kind of school choice today. Parent triggers – laws that allow parents to petition to have their local public schools shut down or be converted into charter schools, or to receive scholarships to send their children to private schools of their choice – are a step beyond charter schools. Seven states have parent triggers so far.

More transformational than either charter schools or parent triggers are vouchers (or scholarships). Such programs allow parents to choose any school, public or private, for their children and public funds follow the students to the schools they attend. The competition and choice made possible by scholarship programs now operating in 26 states is improving the academic achievement of hundreds of thousands of children. Indiana's adoption of a statewide scholarship program promises to extend the benefits to millions of students. Education savings accounts take the idea of vouchers or scholarships a step further by allowing parents to assemble a portfolio of schools, teachers, online courses, and testing services as unique as their children, and to pay for those services out of a savings account similar to their individual retirement account or health savings account. Small pilot programs in Arizona, Louisiana, and Utah point the way for this reform.

Among the principal obstacles to increasing the use of rewards in public education are educators and elected officials who refuse to believe incentives and rewards can work in education. Often they are aided by interest groups such as teachers unions and school administrators who oppose any changes that might negatively affect their current authority and careers. Parents, policymakers, and committed educators must unite to overcome opposition to the use of effective reward programs in the nation's schools.

We hope this book inspires parents to make greater use of properly designed rewards at home as part of their all-important roles as their children's first and only truly life-long teachers. We hope educators will re-examine their views on the use of rewards in their classrooms and come away convinced, as we are, that rewards are an essential tool for instilling the habits and skills students need to succeed in school and beyond. Finally, we hope policymakers will work with parents and educators to remove the roadblocks to a greater use of rewards in education by adopting or expanding policies such as tests with rewards, performance-based pay for teachers, digital learning, and school choice.

With so much at stake, and with so much research readily at hand pointing to the right solutions, why wait any longer?

About the Authors

Herbert J. Walberg

Herbert J. Walberg, Ph.D., is a distinguished visiting fellow at the Hoover Institution and a member of the Koret Task Force on K–12 Education. He holds a Ph.D. from the University of Chicago and taught for 35 years at Harvard University and the University of Illinois at Chicago. Author or editor of more than 75 books, he has written extensively for educational, psychological, and policy journals on measuring and raising student achievement and human accomplishments.

Dr. Walberg's most recent books include *School Choice: The Findings* (Cato Institute, 2007), *Advancing Student Achievement* (EducationNext Books, 2010), and *Tests, Testing, and Genuine School Reform* (EducationNext Books, 2011).

During the past two decades, Walberg has concentrated on educational policy. By invitation, he advised the United Nations, the Organization for Economic Cooperation and Development, and the governments of Israel, Japan, Portugal, Sweden, the U.K., and the U.S. on education research and policy. He was appointed by the U.S. Secretary of Education to the Governing Board of the National Assessment of Educational Progress, and by the President to the National Board for Educational Sciences. He was chosen a fellow by the American Association for the Advancement of Science, the American Psychological Association, the International Academy of Education, and the Royal Statistical Society (U.K.). He chairs the boards of The Heartland Institute and the Beck Foundation.

Joseph L. Bast

Joseph L. Bast is president and CEO of The Heartland Institute, a national nonprofit research and education organization founded in 1984. He is the publisher of *School Reform News* and four other national monthly publications, each sent to every national and state elected official in the United States.

Bast is the author or editor of 22 books, including four books on school reform with coauthor Herbert Walberg: *We Can Rescue Our Children* (1988), *Rebuilding America's Schools* (1991), *Education and Capitalism* (2003), and *Let's Put Parents Back in Charge* (2003). He has written more than a dozen policy studies published by The Heartland Institute on various aspects of school finance and reform. His writing on school reform has appeared in the following peer-reviewed journals: *Cato Journal*, *Economics of Education Review*, *Independent Review*, *Journal of Private Enterprise*, *Journal of School Choice*, and *Phi Delta Kappan*.

Bast has been recognized many times for his contributions to public policy research and debate, including being named one of "The 88 to Watch in 1988" by the *Chicago Tribune* and being awarded the 1994 Roe Award by State Policy Network, the 1996 Sir Antony Fisher International Memorial Award, the 1998 Eagle Award by Eagle Forum, and the 2004 Champion of Liberty Award by the Libertarian National Committee. He was commissioned a Kentucky Colonel by Gov. Paul E. Patton in 1996, elected a member of the Philadelphia Society in 2002, and elected to the boards of directors of the American Conservative Union in 2007.

Index